D1241879

Caribbean
Volunteers
at War

In memory of Flight Lieutenant John J. Blair, DFC,
Jamaica & 102 (Ceylon) Squadron, RAF Bomber
Command and the 500 other Caribbean aircrew volunteers
who flew alongside him.

Lest we forget

'*The application of force alone, without moral support based on a spiritual concept, can never bring about the destruction of an idea or arrest the propagation of it, unless one is ready and able ruthlessly to exterminate the last upholders of that idea even to a man, and also wipe out any tradition which it may tend to leave behind.*'

Adolf Hitler, Mein Kampf (My Struggle)

Caribbean Volunteers at War

The Forgotten Story of Britain's own "Tuskegee Airmen"

By Mark Johnson

Pen & Sword
AVIATION

First published in Great Britain in 2014 by
Pen & Sword Aviation
an imprint of
Pen & Sword Books Ltd
47 Church Street
Barnsley
South Yorkshire
S70 2AS

Copyright © Mark Johnson 2014

ISBN 978 1 78346 291 9

Typeset in Ehrhardt by
Mac Style, Bridlington, East Yorkshire
Printed and bound in the UK by CPI Group (UK) Ltd, Croydon,
CRO 4YY

Pen & Sword Books Ltd incorporates the imprints of Pen & Sword
Archaeology, Atlas, Aviation, Battleground, Discovery, Family History,
History, Maritime, Military, Naval, Politics, Railways, Select, Transport,
True Crime, and Fiction, Frontline Books, Leo Cooper, Praetorian
Press, Seaforth Publishing and Wharncliffe.

For a complete list of Pen & Sword titles please contact
PEN & SWORD BOOKS LIMITED
47 Church Street, Barnsley, South Yorkshire, S70 2AS, England
E-mail: enquiries@pen-and-sword.co.uk
Website: www.pen-and-sword.co.uk

Contents

Author's Note

Growing up in London during the early 1960s, the scars of Adolf Hitler's rampage across Europe and North Africa during the Second World War were all around me. The gaps in the buildings and the old bomb sites, the comic books and films, the old men's tales, the absent relatives and the still fresh recollections of our parents and grandparents made the events of twenty years before feel like memories we all shared.

The British had their war thrust upon them and my mother's family included a Royal Engineer officer who served in Italy and France, a Home Guard volunteer and several Dutch relatives who were killed by the Nazis during the occupation of the Netherlands. On my father's side we are Jamaican and for many years I assumed that this side of the family had little or no connection with the war at all.

When I was twelve, we moved to Jamaica to live and I finished high school there. It was in Jamaica that I first met my great-uncle (my paternal grandmother's brother), former Royal Air Force Flight Lieutenant John J. Blair, DFC. A distinguished but extremely modest and soft spoken Jamaican gentleman, once a school teacher, but by then practicing law, great-uncle John never spoke of the war, or of his wartime service, but over time I gleaned snippets of his past from other relatives. Ever so slowly, a picture of a black RAF volunteer who had flown a full tour with RAF Bomber Command over Germany between late 1944 and the spring of 1945, and who had earned a Distinguished Flying Cross in the process, started to emerge and I decided that I had to record his tale.

I completed my own military service in the small but operationally active Jamaica Defence Force, where our focus was on interdicting the international narcotics trade through and from the island. I like to believe that it was this fact that encouraged great-uncle John to finally tell me his story. 'How did you get him to talk?' was the question posed by several of my other relatives. John Blair spoke to me for many hours and I recorded it all on tape. From the resulting transcript, my follow-up research and interviews with other

Jamaican RAF veterans, I realized for the first time that he was only one of thousands of Caribbean volunteers to join up for European service in the early 1940s. I also discovered that as many as 500 of these men had become aircrew and over a third of those had been killed in action, or, in a few cases, had actually been taken prisoner by the Germans, while another fifty men had succeeded in joining the RAF as aircrew from West Africa. I learned in addition that female RAF volunteers had travelled to England from the Caribbean for ground duties and that the first black woman in British military uniform was also a West Indian.

These were startling discoveries, for never throughout my upbringing in England, or during my schooling in Jamaica, had I heard any mention of these amazing individualists. Never in all the reading I had done on the topic of the Second World War, and it was extensive, had the subject received so much as a single mention. What had inspired these people to go and fight? Where had they served? Who had died, how, and in what numbers? How had black men survived in the Stalag Luft system, the network of prisoner-of-war camps built by the German Air Force specifically for Allied aircrew? What other challenges had the volunteers needed to overcome? What had become of them once the fighting was over and why, when films like *The Tuskegee Airmen* (1995) and Red Tails (2012) had received international attention, were the men of the black dominions, who flew in equally large numbers, not properly recognized and celebrated, either at home in the Caribbean, or in Britain? These and other questions nagged me.

So I began my search for answers, a search that has taken almost two decades. During this process I discovered a great deal that I did not know and my attitudes towards our shared colonial history, race and racism, and the actions of Bomber Command itself, were challenged in many ways. I also came to understand that the true role of the military historian is not merely to recount the dates and times and places, the words of the generals, the tonnages dropped, the machines and their statistics, but to give a voice to the dead, the unheard and the forgotten. It is to tell the story of the many; to describe not the just the courage of the medal winners, but also war's horrors and its victims, so that later generations may have some chance of avoiding the mistakes of their ancestors.

The story of the Caribbean and West African RAF crews during the Second World War is a tale rarely told and even less frequently heard, and contrary to popular belief, many of the volunteers who were successful in their efforts to join the RAF as pilots, signallers, wireless operators, navigators, or air gunners, did not come from affluent, or even middle class backgrounds. But despite having often grown up in what counted for poverty by most European standards – even grinding poverty in some cases – the volunteers had equipped themselves for military service through education, hard work and personal commitment and they would succeed in overcoming the multiple barriers of class, race, politics and geography to join the RAF, complete their training with flying colours and fly operationally against Hitler's veteran airmen. That they came knocking on the door of the British Air Ministry, a systemically racist organization at the time, is a marvel in itself. What they subsequently achieved during their collective service is nothing less than astounding.

Acknowledgements

T oo many people have contributed to this work for me to thank every one of them individually and I apologize to any who are not singled out here. Your help has not been forgotten. Very special thanks must go to Wing Commander Jez Holmes of II (AC) Squadron, Royal Air Force, who quite literally took me and my project under his wing when he learned of it and who not only arranged for me to visit his unit at RAF Marham and review their Second World War operational logs and photos, but who also went out of his way to introduce me to other still active RAF Squadrons in which West Indians had served. Jez Holmes has very kindly contributed the Foreword to this book and he is mentioned again in the Epilogue.

During my visit to Marham I was delighted to meet three very impressive RAF officers who guided me through the logs and showed me around the base and its aircraft. My heartfelt thanks therefore go to Flight Lieutenants Deborah (Debs) Borrie and Geoff Williams of II (AC) Squadron and Flight Lieutenant Richard (Rich) Woods of IX (Bomber) Squadron for their warm welcome and very kind assistance.

I would also like to thank Louis Brozinic for her help with the online aspects of my research and for compiling the list of Caribbean aircrew that appears at the end of the book. I also want to thank the administrators of and contributors to the various websites listed under Sources, without whose efforts our research would have been far more difficult to carry out, as well as Neil Webster for taking the time to search through thousands of operational logs to find examples of missions my subjects took part in.

Also, I must acknowledge Jerome Lee, a driving force behind the online compilation of profiles of the Caribbean volunteers who very kindly shared many links to historical documents and other sources with me and Audrey Dewjee of Yorkshire, who has been researching the West Indian contribution to the war effort for many years and was able to point me in the right direction on a number of occasions.

One of the triggers for this book was another work titled *Lancaster W4827: failed to return*, written by Joost Klootwijk and translated by Hans Klootwijk. This tells the story of the aircraft in which Cy Grant, who features prominently in my account, flew to war. Hans also administers the primary online resource Caribbean Aircrew (see Online Resources at the end of the book) and he has been a tremendous help during the course of my own project.

Finally, I must say a big 'thank you' to Petra, Cleo and Luca for putting up with my long absences upstairs in my study and my ceaseless tapping on my keyboard.

Prologue

When the cry of alarm came, it shocked every member of the crew; 'Starboard outer engine on fire, Skipper!' The voice of the mid-upper gunner was distorted by the intercom, but still recognizable. The aircraft had been hit! The pilot dived steeply in an effort to smother the blaze, but when he levelled out, the crew, peering through their perspex windows and turrets, could see the flames spreading rapidly. All eyes were fixed on the burning wing and on the outermost engine, which was trailing flames, sparks and black smoke behind the wounded aircraft. Suddenly, one of the wheels of the undercarriage fell away, a flaming circle of rubber that plummeted towards the black surface of the earth 20,000 feet below like a meteor, down through the night sky, its own trail of flame and sparks marking its route and heralding their likely fate.

The crew, flying only their third operational mission, knew that their survival was growing less likely with every passing second. By the time they reached the Dutch North Sea coast, they were a fiery comet lancing across the sky high above Holland. Countless pairs of watching eyes were also focused on them from below, where Dutchmen and German occupiers alike would have been transfixed by the struggle of the dying bird. The fire had quickly spread to the fuselage and from there across to the other wing, and the heat and flames were driving the crew towards the front of the plane where they huddled. Still airborne, the interior of the aircraft was an inferno that nobody could penetrate. Even the aluminium airframe was now burning. The navigator had given the pilot the shortest course to England, but both men knew they were flying into a headwind of 80 miles an hour and that it was unlikely they could make it across the cold black waters of the North Sea before the plane had burned to a cinder or exploded in mid-air.

Although the crew had unanimously agreed to risk getting across the water rather than turning back and bailing out over occupied territory in the event of just such a crisis, it was becoming extremely difficult to control the bomber. Finally, the pilot decided to turn back over land after all. And just in time, for no sooner had he forced the nose of the struggling Lancaster around than the aircraft pitched down again and they began to rapidly lose their remaining altitude. Reluctantly, he bowed to the inevitable and gave the order, 'Well, guys, this is it, bail out and good luck. Get to it!'

The navigator, Cy Grant, moved forward towards the escape hatch in the bomb-aimer's compartment. Although the risks were known to all fliers, he now realized that he had never contemplated actually being in this situation. In his mind, this was always something that happened to other people – he was somehow immune. Like every crew, this one had been instructed in the use of parachutes, but they had never had to practice actually bailing out of an aircraft and the navigator had to force himself to focus on the procedure.

When Grant arrived in the nose of the Lancaster, he found that the bomb aimer and the flight engineer, Ronald Hollywood, who should already have jumped, were struggling to get through the small hatch in the floor, encumbered as they were with their bulky flight gear and parachutes. The pilot now left his controls and came after them and the four crew members were soon piled one on top of the other, tossed from side to side in the cramped space as the aircraft began to meander across the sky. The flames were rapidly approaching this last remaining section of the plane and the heat was intense. Inside, the fire roared as it consumed 1,000 gallons of aviation fuel and heavy machine gun ammunition exploded with repeated loud bangs. Outside, the freezing air screamed past.

Grant couldn't understand why he was unable to escape but he felt neither fear nor panic, despite the heat of the fire on his back. He was locked in a timeless moment of inertia. Everything was happening in slow motion when suddenly, with a deafening blast that seemed to light up the whole sky, the aircraft exploded and disintegrated. Freed from their entanglement by the blast and by the rupture of the thin skin of the plane that had held them, the jumble of crewmen began a tumbling free-fall into eternity, all entwined one moment, alone in the vast black silence of the sky the next.

Suddenly, Grant's parachute opened. He felt a sudden jerk and the pressure of the harness as the wind snatched at the canopy. Although he was unaware of it having done so, his hand must have pulled the ripcord, guided by another unconscious part of his brain. He was now swaying violently from side to side and, except for the rush of the wind, he was suspended in a dream world of mist and utter silence. There was a sense of unreality, for he experienced no sensation of descending.

Slowly, he became aware of distant searchlights and the glow of a fire far below him. Was that his aircraft? Where were the other members of the crew? There wasn't another parachute anywhere in sight. The night sky, which had been home to a stream of several hundred aircraft, was now seemingly empty and eerily silent. He appeared to be drifting aimlessly, neither rising nor falling, with the only sound the wind swelling the silk of the open parachute above him. For some moments he imagined that it was lifting him upwards, gently conveying him away to heaven. Perhaps he was dead? Then all of a sudden he sensed the rush of an immense shadow coming towards him at terrific speed from below. It was the ground reaching up to gather him in bruisingly. The date was 26 June 1943 and Cy Grant was the rarest of things – a black West Indian RAF volunteer, blown out of his exploding aircraft alive over Nazi occupied Europe.

Foreword

Wing Commander Jez Holmes MA RAF,
Officer Commanding No. II (Army Cooperation) Squadron

I am writing this foreword on the 15 September 2013, Battle of Britain day, a day that commemorates the sacrifices of the 'Few', seventy-three years on from the Royal Air Force's most famous victory. I am also incredibly proud to say that I was present at the unveiling of the Bomber Command Memorial on the 28 June 2012, which commemorates the 55,573 airmen of Bomber Command who lost their lives in the Second World War – a sobering number when one considers that only 125,000 men flew those missions deep into enemy territory. With survival rates lower than infantry officers in the trenches of the First World War, it took a special type of person to climb into those aircraft night after night. By chance, during my MA studies at the Defence Academy of the United Kingdom, I came across a small group of the Second World War airmen that took that bravery to a new level.

Although the British Empire would eventually be one of the catalysts for modern multicultural Britain, at its height in the late nineteenth and early twentieth century racially driven discriminatory policies and attitudes were societal norms in the British ruled dominions and colonies. I chose to study the British Empire at the Defence Academy to fill a hole in my knowledge, and being an airman I was naturally interested in the development of air power through this period. During my research I gradually began to uncover extraordinary stories of individuals who, often at their expense and under their own steam, travelled the world to join the Royal Air Force and fight the might of the Third Reich. Their stories were not only extraordinary for the distance that they travelled, or the commitment that they showed, but also because they were West Indian, they were African and they were from Asia – these men had to fight to be allowed to fight. Their stories were difficult to find with very few books or studies on the matter even though many were well educated, going on to become lawyers and politicians. I was therefore surprised when Mark Johnson asked me if I knew of the story of the Jamaican airmen of the Second World War – I met Mark when he was a guest at a Dining-In night at the Officers' Mess, Royal Air Force Marham. We would go on to discuss at length the amazing history that he has captured with such clarity, bringing to life the hardship of the journeys and the sheer terror of the sorties.

I command a current 'Bomber' Squadron of the Royal Air Force, No. II (Army Cooperation) Squadron, and I have completed six operational tours of duty flying the Tornado GR1 and GR4 – few in the modern military lack warfighting experience. Much of the context today is different – the threat, the targets, the precision, what kind of warfare is acceptable to society, and of course the modern Royal Air Force is a proud equal opportunities employer. Losses of the scale suffered in the air during the Second World War are difficult to comprehend now, as is the bravery of those that faced them. The Royal Air Force will reach its centenary in 2018 and has a rich history – Mark Johnson has uncovered and captured one of the forgotten elements of that history, allowing us to give thanks to those who made the ultimate sacrifice in our name.

Chapter 1

Island Life

At 2242 hours on the night of 25 June 1943, the first bomber of Cy Grant's 103 Squadron, Royal Air Force, had taken off from its base at Elsham Wolds in North Lincolnshire with its human cargo of seven crew members and its explosive cargo of 9,000lbs of bombs and incendiaries, plus 2,000 gallons of potentially explosive aviation fuel. The destination of this flying bomb was the Ruhr, Germany's industrial heartland, where it would drop its massive load onto the factories and houses of the town of Gelsenkirchen.

One by one, the heavily laden 103 Squadron bombers, twenty-four in total, lumbered up into the darkness, circling and gathering, half blind, and then heading off to merge with the other 449 aircraft of Bomber Command detailed to take part in the raid. Thirty RAF bombers would be lost that night, representing a 6.7 per cent casualty rate, significantly above the 5 per cent nightly loss regarded as acceptable by Bomber Command's leadership.

Born in what was then British Guiana (now British Guyana), which forms a part of the South American mainland, Grant was amongst the first volunteers from the Caribbean colonies to join up. The son of an austere, bookish, but kindly Moravian minister, he had grown up surrounded by friends and neighbours of African, East Indian, Dutch, French and Portuguese extraction. Grant did not yet class himself as black, that being a derogatory term at that time in his homeland, but rather as 'coloured' or 'brown-skinned'. His own father was half-Scot and half-Barbadian, while his mother was part East Indian. His parents had met on the island of Antigua in the Lesser Antilles, part of an emerald necklace of islands that separates the Caribbean Sea from the Atlantic Ocean. Cy's grandfather had been one of several generations of Scotsmen who left their homeland to make new homes for themselves in every part of the Empire and who quickly became a cornerstone of its foundations, while his mother's Indian ancestors had come to the region as indentured labourers to fill the gaps left by the workers who had abandoned the sugar plantations when slavery was abolished in the British dominions in the 1830s.

The Caribbean was and remains to this day a patchwork of complex multi-racial, multi-cultural societies and British Guyana was no exception. Each Caribbean nation has its own particular mix of peoples and over generations this has given the inhabitants different features, hues, languages or accents, mannerisms and traditions. While diets were largely based on the same ingredients, styles of cooking varied widely between the islands and those countries on the South and Central American mainland that counted themselves as either Caribbean or West Indian. Notwithstanding the majority African population in many locations, Native American, East Indian, Chinese, Spanish, British, French, Dutch and several other influences took cuisine and culture in different directions. In Trinidad and British Guyana, where as much as half the population is of East Indian extraction, these differences are even more pronounced than elsewhere in the region.

Cy Grant had little reason to mix closely with the East Indian and African labouring class of British Guyana, not to mention the wraith-like 'Buck Indians' (the indigenous Amerindian population). He only discovered his blackness when he arrived in England and it was firmly pointed out to him. While Grant was standing one day outside an RAF building, a polite, well spoken middle aged Englishman approached him and they started to chat amiably. The man expressed surprise that Grant's English was as good as his own and for the first time in his life Cy Grant started to become aware of his own foreignness and the fact that it was actually British Guyana and not Britain that was his mother country. In 1941, Grant was only aware that, 'The unbroken flatness of the physical landscape, along with a pervading sense of colonial stagnation seemed to impose limits on my future horizons. I had to escape.'

The original European arrivals in the region had in fact shunned British Guyana's flood plains, deeming them too difficult to tame and completely lacking in promise. But when the Dutch arrived they immediately put their expertise in reclaiming and protecting low-lying land to good use and British Guyana – meaning 'land of many rivers' in the language of its indigenous inhabitants – soon boasted a sophisticated network of canals and dykes. The now valuable sugar producing flatlands were to change hands multiple times, with the French, Dutch, British and others vying for control, but by 1940 the country was firmly established as a part of the British Empire and it was also a nation with one of the highest literacy rates in the world. In the forests, however, the descendants of the surviving indigenous tribes lurked, hiding from the foreign invaders and the deadly diseases they had brought with them, which had decimated the peoples of the entire continent.

One aspect of the spirit of that time and place is captured in a tale Grant told of his father. A strictly religious man, but also a fanatical cricket fan, Mr Grant Snr had read in the newspaper that a friendly match was planned between the West Indies cricket team and British Guyana's national side for the following day, which was a Sunday. The next morning, saying nothing to his family, Mr Grant headed off to the cricket ground early, carrying only an umbrella and his bible. Once at the ground, instead of taking his usual seat in the stands, the Minister walked out to the middle of the pitch, opened his umbrella as protection against the sun, and occupied the area of play, still clutching the Holy Book. Neither umpires nor players ventured out of the pavilion to confront him and the crowd that had assembled eventually gave up any hope of seeing a game and dispersed. The sanctity of the Lord's Day had been protected and the rugged individualism that still characterizes so many Caribbean people has no better example.

By 1945, more than 6,000 black and coloured Caribbean volunteers had joined the Royal Air Force for service in the European theatre of war. More than 400 of these men would serve as aircrew, flying and fighting in the skies over Nazi occupied Europe and deep into the airspace of Germany itself. At least 100 of those aircrew volunteers were eventually commissioned as officers, something that had been officially prohibited before the war commenced, and 251 served with the rank of sergeant or above, according to the RAF records. (RAF Memo S.7. (Cent.) 20.2.45.) A large percentage of the aircrew volunteers would also be decorated for their courageous service. (Cy Grant states that 103 Caribbean aircrew volunteers were decorated.) At least one third of the volunteers are believed to have been killed in action, although the fates of many others have not yet been confirmed and the true death toll is probably higher.

In 1945 the RAF attempted to collect, after the fact, statistics on the numbers of 'coloured' RAF aircrew serving up to 20 February 1945. While the list is incomplete, it does arrive at a total of 282 coloured aircrew from the Caribbean region. The gap between this figure and my own estimate of 500 is explained by the potential for my list to include a few men of pure British descent who would not be included in the RAF list, along with the fact that the war in Europe still had three months left to run, and the war against Japan six months, when the RAF survey was conducted, providing ample opportunity for many more aircrew to arrive through the training pipeline.

The RAF volunteers came from all walks of life and all parts of the Caribbean. John Ebanks was born in the poor rural parish of St Elizabeth in western Jamaica in 1920. This remote fragment of the vast British Empire was a tough, drought stricken place where families barely got by through farming and fishing. The hot sun beat down on the dusty red soil, almost desert-like in its appearance and a future source of alumina for large North American mining firms, but nothing more than a source of irritation for the local women attempting to keep the floors and furniture of their small wooden houses or thatched roof cottages clean and tidy.

After Trinidad, the island of Jamaica would supply the largest contingent of black volunteers to the Royal Air Force from the Caribbean. Like British Guyana, Jamaica's complex social composition is the product of invasion, epidemic disease, genocide, slavery, revolt, colonial rule and marital or other relations between peoples of different ethnicity and class; between master and slave, overseer and indentured labourer, black, white, East Indian and Chinese. Jamaica and its indigenous Arawak inhabitants had been discovered for Europe in 1494 by Christopher Columbus, during his second voyage to the Americas. Financed by King Ferdinand and Queen Isabella of Spain, the Italian adventurer had promised to find Spain a safe route to the treasures and markets of India and the Orient, thus avoiding the dangers and taxation associated with existing routes via Ottoman lands and the famed 'Silk Road'.

The powerful royal couple had already completed the re-conquest of the Iberian Peninsula from the Muslim Moors, forcing those remaining in the territory to convert to Catholicism (the 'converso Moriscos' in Spanish,

Colony or country	Coloured Aircrew
Jamaica	126
Trinidad	82
Leeward and Windward Islands	24
British Guyana	21
Barbados	12
British Honduras	10
Bermuda	1
B.W.I. (island not specified)	1
Aruba	1
Bahamas	4
Total	282

Table 1: RAF table of estimated number of coloured aircrew as at 20 February 1945. My composite table of names in the Appendix suggests a total of at least 440, and possibly as many as 500. Note that the term 'coloured' is the one used by the RAF in its records.

from which the French name Maurice derives). With their conquests in the Americas, they would now elevate the reunited but impoverished Kingdom of Spain almost to superpower status, although subsequent leaders would fail to maintain that supremacy.

It might easily be said that it was in fact the Arawaks who discovered Columbus when they walked down their beaches to meet him, as their forbears had taken a far longer journey from Asia via Alaska and North America to the Caribbean and South America, where they colonized the continent for the first time. But history belongs to the victors and within a few short years these Arawaks would all be dead, most killed by the diseases brought by the Europeans and their animals, including the ship's rats, the remainder hunted down and slain by the Spanish for sport during a campaign of ethnic cleansing.

Jamaica, the name being a bastardization of the Arawak name Xaymaca, which means 'land of wood and water', would become a strategically important Spanish base and later, the jewel in the crown of British West

Indian possessions, producing large quantities of high grade sugar and tobacco, cultivated on great plantations that exploited the free labour of forcibly imported West African slaves. During the period of the slave trade in the Americas, no less than eleven million Africans would be shipped across the Atlantic to be sold in local slave markets and millions more would be born in bondage, the descendants of those international arrivals. After Britain's loss of most of its North American settlements, resulting from her defeat in the American War of Independence and the formation of the United States of America, Jamaica would assume even greater strategic importance; as we shall see.

The role of black soldiers within, or in conflict with, European and American armies and navies evolved in parallel with the trade in slaves. Black rebels, some escaped slaves themselves and others slaves in revolt, fought the colonizers on several Caribbean islands. In the case of Haiti these rebels actually won their independence from the French. Meanwhile, the Jamaican Maroons, descendants of slaves belonging to the Spanish who had been abandoned by their owners when the British invaded the island in 1655, also fought the British Regiments to a standstill in the hilly jungle terrain of the interior and they were able to negotiate a formal peace treaty of their own that gave them independence within a large reservation in the mountainous heart of the country. This quasi-independent status remains in place to the current day.

In the United States, black troops were inducted into the armies of both sides during the American Civil War and others were engaged after the war as so-called 'Buffalo Soldiers' (allegedly a reference to their skin colour by their adversaries), to fight as mounted infantry against the native American tribes in the west during another great power genocidal expansionary period.

Not all colonial representatives were unsympathetic towards the colonized peoples of the Empire. Tom Forsyth was a Canadian soldier stationed in Jamaica between 1940–1941 and his well-written diary provides us with numerous insights into military life at the time, the land itself, the nature of Jamaican society and politics, and the perspectives of one of its occupiers:

'The Jamaica Infantry Volunteers and our men were roused out of bed (at Up Park Camp, Kingston) at five by the bugle sounding stand to. Agitation among the working people; they may strike for an eight hour day. A strike means a riot here, so all ranks are confined to barracks to be in readiness for action…

'Got a sixpence worth of limes which are a miniature lemon orange and scrounged some sugar at the sergeants' mess, and using ice water from the block of ice which comes each morning, made us a good drink… The tea on this island is now five shillings a pound and the flour for our bread is being adulterated by adding corn meal. This makes it very heavy and it does not rise properly. The best flour never came here anyway… The two (Jamaican) Royal Engineers who maintain the big tennis court here were cooking their dinner of rice and peas, flavoured with milk squeezed by hand out of freshly grated coconut meat and added spices… Goonga peas grow on a plant like a young tree, Paw Paws on a tall tree, pineapple and sweet potatoes (also)… The poinsettia grows here like a large shrub or bush, about three feet high, all around the NAAFI. It is in full bloom, very ornamental. Bob Grace said this would be a wonderful country if we were not in the army, and if there were no black people here. I said there are too many "ifs" in that statement …

'The Chinese and the Hindus own the large business concerns here. They work hard and are very astute managers and directors of free enterprise…

'Tonight the sergeants are having a dance to celebrate the fact that a year ago we landed in Jamaica. I do not see any logic in that. A lot of (our) men who were once decent human beings have been ruined… Free soup after! It will take more than soup to wash away the infamy from this regiment brought on by Jamaican rum.'

Forsythe also described the wild boars that live in the mountains. They are not indigenous and are descended from domestic pigs that arrived with the Spanish occupiers and then escaped into the hills. Over many generations they reverted to their original form, growing large tusks and dangerous teeth. A mature boar is potentially lethal as the animals are omnivorous and have been known to kill and consume adult men. When I was stationed in the Blue Mountains, training Jamaica Defence Force infantry recruits in the 1980s, the boars were still present in numbers and were hunted for their flesh by local people. I was told by some Maroons that if injured, the animal was known to play possum, waiting for the hunter to approach then jumping up and attacking him. On one occasion, a boar dragged one of our soldiers out of our jungle camp by his foot at night while the man was sleeping and we had to give chase, grab the trooper and play tug of war for him. He was unharmed, but the whole toecap of his heavy leather army boot had been ripped clean away by the boar's teeth. The local crocodiles (in fact, they are Caimans) are another story and there is no playing tug of war with them!

Its large natural harbour and central position in the Caribbean – astride the routes between the oilfields of South America and the United States East Coast and close to shipping routes through the strategically vital Panama Canal – meant that Jamaica had long been the main British naval base in the region. Indeed, the strategic importance of the island was recognized hundreds of years earlier when it served as the base of operations for the notorious privateer, Henry Morgan, during his campaign against the Spanish, and later as Admiral Nelson's regional headquarters during his prolonged hunt for the French fleet. The main city on the island and its unofficial capital, Port Royal, 'storehouse and treasury of the West Indies' and 'the wickedest city on earth', was destroyed by an earthquake in 1692. This submerged most of the city and the resulting tsunami sank over 400 ships in the harbour. Sitting at the end of the narrow peninsula that bounds Kingston's harbour and with two thirds of its buildings gone beneath the waters, it was then gutted by a fire in 1703 and what little was left was badly knocked about by a hurricane in 1722. The remaining settlement at Port Royal was struck once more by a strong earthquake in 1907. To this day, the place has yet to recover from these calamities and the resulting lack of investment. It is an impoverished, dusty backwater, whose only claims to fame are a small museum, diving opportunities amongst the sunken ruins and walks along the parapet of the surviving fort. There is also excellent seafood to be had at the local restaurants.

Despite abandoning Port Royal itself, Royal Navy ships nevertheless sailed from Kingston Harbour in December 1939 to engage the heavy cruiser *Admiral Graf Spee* when she made her fateful voyage along the South

American coast toward her final battle near the mouth of the River Plate and her eventual scuttling at Montevideo. From 1941 onwards, the US Navy operated a seaplane base from Little Goat Island, on Jamaica's south coast, for the purpose of detecting and sinking the German U-boats that infested those waters, and hundreds of German sailors would later be held prisoner at camps in Kingston and elsewhere on the island. Jamaica was therefore very much involved in the Second World War from an early date.

With five brothers and six sisters, John Ebanks came from a very traditional Jamaican family background characterized by discipline, hard work and a focus on educational achievement as the key to self-improvement. All the same, when John decided in late 1941 to join the Royal Air Force, he didn't tell his parents what he was planning to do until he had already been accepted by the recruiting board.

John's father was a teacher, as were the parents of many volunteers and many of the volunteers themselves. The Ebanks family shared the ancestral history of a large part of Jamaican society, being descended from a mixture of slaves, slave owners, or foreign adventurers, who, in the Ebanks' case, took the form of a pair of brothers from Scotland named Eubanks. The brothers had decided to leave their father's carpet making business and follow in the footsteps of Columbus. For those with the time to search online, antique Eubank or Ewbank Carpet Sweeper machines can still be found for sale. Boarding a ship sometime in the early-to-mid 1800s, the Eubanks brothers eventually reached the Cayman Islands, where one of them settled. The second brother continued on his journey, but his ship ran into a storm and he was shipwrecked on the south-west coast of Jamaica, at a place called Treasure Beach. Generations later, the Ebanks family of Treasure Beach, in south St Elizabeth, was a well-established part of local society, contributing to the phalanx of local teachers, nurses, clerks and junior administrators that delivered many of the key services required in an early twentieth century community.

Very close by, in the adjacent community of Pedro Plains, the future Flight Lieutenant John Blair was also born into a family of teachers. There were eight children and he was the youngest. Erudite and bloody-minded, the Blairs were not to be trifled with and they too provided a string of successful farmers, educators, nurses, doctors, military men and lawyers over successive generations, who would serve at all levels in Jamaican society. John, much more soft spoken and milder mannered than most Blairs, was apparently a surprise to his parents, 'coming out of the blue' as he put it, and the sibling he followed was a full seven years older.

Life in rural Jamaica at that time moved at a very slow pace. As elsewhere in the region, there were no motor vehicles, no televisions or radios, indeed no electricity, nor anything that depended on it. John's farming and fishing community was labour intensive and it employed techniques that went back centuries. The men tilled their fields by hand, or with the help of a beast of burden, while the fishermen cast their nets and set their lobster pots from canoes. After work, dominoes were played on makeshift wooden tables, the players slamming the winning pieces down loudly, making the pieces already on the table jump several inches into the air. Rum and beer were the main drinks, but drunks were the exception and much maligned, while the better in society would not be seen dead in a local bar. Women cooked, cleaned, scrubbed and cared for their children, while those same children scampered down the dusty lanes, chased by mongrel dogs, stoning mango trees for fruit where they saw it and conversing as loudly as children everywhere. The mangoes came in all shapes, flavours and sizes. Number 7, Number 11, Bombay, East Indian, Hayden and Julie were the most highly prized types, having the best taste and being much larger and less stringy than the Common, Blackey or Hairy varieties most often consumed by the children. Beefy Mango was the largest kind, almost the size of a small pineapple, but this variety was rare and few of the children had ever seen one. Several other types of mango could be found at different locations around the island, perhaps twenty-five in total, but few people could name them all. Not one of these mangoes was indigenous. They had all been brought to the region and planted deliberately by its European colonizers, along with a wide range of other plants now synonymous with the West Indies, including rice, peas, breadfruit and sugar cane.

Jamaican life followed the seasons and was further marked by the big events of birth, marriage, sickness and death, with church going for all on Sundays and Holy Days. Serious pastors and stern-faced church going ladies wore their Sunday best, complete with hats and white gloves, while the men turned out in dark suits in the ninety degree heat, pulling their unwilling offspring along with them. Twisted ears and spanked bottoms could be expected by any children who protested too loudly. Numerous hymns and prayers accompanied long sermons and readings from the Bible. Nervous young men and women would experience their first public speaking engagement on such occasions, but from these inauspicious beginnings many a great orator or singer would emerge.

Bob Marley was born in rural Jamaica in 1945, the son of a white plantation overseer, (said by some to hail from Sussex and by others from Ireland) by then in his late fifties, and an 18-year-old Jamaican village girl. Marley's early life experiences will have followed a similar line to those described.

The national sports in the West Indies, the parts of the Caribbean ruled by Britain, were cricket and athletics. When not playing 'back yard cricket' in the dirt behind their houses, or in the lanes, youngsters would gather in the shade beneath their verandas to play 'nail cricket' in the dirt, with two inch nails representing the players and a marble serving as the ball. Football was also played, but not to the same degree, while sports such as rugby, tennis and golf were the exclusive domain of the privileged. This has remained true almost to the present day, although the range of modern sports has expanded, in part due to the influence of American culture and the granting of sports scholarships by US colleges to many West Indian youths.

In addition to mangoes, pineapples, cashews, peanuts, guinep or 'Spanish Lime' (a fruit with a very large seed and little meat), curried goat or chicken, fried fish, bammy (a flat bread made from cassava – an Arawak creation), ackee (a fruit cooked as a vegetable), salt fish shipped down from Canada, sugar cane and its products, breadfruits (descended from those carried to the island from the Pacific by men such as Captain Bligh), bananas, dumplings made of a mix of boiled flour and cornmeal or fried dumplings called Johnny Cakes (from 'journey cake'), avocado pears, yams, sweet potatoes, maize (known locally as 'corn') and a wide variety of other tropical foods made up the Jamaican diet. Largely viewed as poor man's food, even slave food, these staples would one day come to be regarded as delicacies by the Jamaican communities that eventually made their homes abroad in Britain and North America. The other islands all consumed variations of this diet.

Before the arrival of refrigerated transport, various parts of Jamaica specialized in particular ingredients or recipes. Jerked Pork (smoked and highly seasoned) could only really be obtained in the Parish of Portland in the north-east, fish was available anywhere, but bammy was best eaten in the south, particularly St Elizabeth. The south was also the source of peanuts and cashews, the latter growing on large trees and needing to be harvested by hand, one cashew nut at a time, this making them relatively expensive. Sugar and tobacco grew in the south and in parts of the western central region. Roast corn and roast yam could be bought along any major road, as could jelly coconuts, the milk of which was drunk before the nut was split open with one blow from a sharp machete and the soft jelly consumed with a makeshift spoon hacked from the thick skin.

The East Indian migrant population, who had arrived in the wake of emancipation to work on the recently abandoned sugar estates, brought their curries and rice plants with them, while Chinese immigrants also added their cuisine to the mix. In Kingston all of these styles and more, including English and Lebanese, were available: although most residents of the capital were not exposed to such a refined range of alternatives. The British soldiery made Spam and corned beef popular, as they traded their tins for goods and services. Many people thought that eating army food was bound to be beneficial to their health and wellbeing, the soldiers themselves being so big and strong.

To this day, Pedro Plains experiences long, hot, dry periods and the land is open savannah with only a few stunted trees and thorny bushes scattered here and there. At many points sharp limestone rocks stick up out of the ground like little mountain peaks. These characteristics are in stark contrast to the more general lushness that gives Jamaica its name. Travelling the greener parts of the country, Tom Forsythe recalled:

'The road was very dusty and the driving tiresome, but the splendid beach, the lovely scenery around the (Dunns River) falls, the clear, clean river water and the change from camp, made any discomfort all worth it. The country we passed on the way was for the most part flat lands where bananas and sugar cane plantations flourish. However, there was some rolling, grazing country, which was surrounded, divided and subdivided by miles of stone fences.

'On another occasion we drove to Morant Bay, about forty miles from Kingston. We saw some lovely scenery, crossed over five rivers which were either dry or practically dry, but whose wide boulder strewn beds testified to violent raging seasonal floods. We saw Sugar Loaf Mountain, so named for its shape. Part of the road skirts the seashore which is lined with coconut palms. The breakers rolling up and crashing on the beach are a fascinating sight to anyone born on the prairies. We only stopped for a few minutes at Morant Bay, long enough to fix a little trouble on the car; a pin came out of part of the clutch, and we used a bolt out of the body to take its place. On the way back, we stopped at a small village and bought nine large ripe bananas for a penny half penny, and three coconuts for three pence and a farthing. Stopped at Sea View for a soft drink.'

When John Blair was growing up, West Indian rural schools were often tiny facilities comprising a single room for a class made up of children of all ages and controlled by a solitary teacher. Education was delivered in the Victorian style, with the teacher standing at the front of the class teaching, while the children sat at their little wooden tables and recited whatever had just been taught until it was locked in their memories forever. When the children weren't reciting or writing, they kept deathly quiet in order to avoid the thrashing that would be the reward for any whispered comment or other unwelcome sound. Children in such a school did not raise their hands to ask questions – questions were asked of them and they had better know the answer.

Most schools at the time had an active Scout Troop and John Blair could remember the boys parading, smartly dressed in their khaki uniforms, but every one of them barefoot in the dirt. Those children had feet hardened by years of running over stony ground, their soles like thick leather, and it was the wearing of shoes on church days that came as a discomfort. Walking barefoot in all weathers and over all ground was the norm for most and unremarkable. Of course, this wasn't only the case in the Caribbean. During the American Civil War, for example, a majority of the men of the south had marched northward into battle barefoot, a fact rarely captured in the cinematic retelling. The expectation that children would all own one, much less several, decent pairs of shoes is no older than our parents or grandparents in most parts of the world.

As the youngest brother of the school mistress, Jemima Blair, John started school aged five, two years before the normal age of seven. This created some interesting problems when the School Inspector visited. All British colonial government inspectors at that time were Englishmen sent out by Her Majesty's Government to ensure that educational standards were maintained across the Empire and they often delivered this result with great efficiency, this being one of Britain's great gifts to the world. But John and his classmates simply called these inspectors what they called every Englishman; 'white men'. John remembered being pushed out of the back of the building by his sister when one of these white men arrived, so that questions about his age would not get her into trouble.

In spite of these challenges, John Blair and his classmates received a good education, and he eventually qualified as a teacher himself. Tall, athletic and a first-class sprinter, when the time came to volunteer for the Royal Air Force, John Blair would join John Ebanks and many other volunteers, being judged suitable for the most intellectually challenging role available to aircrew, that of navigator.

In addition to his school mistress sister Jemima, John Blair's brothers, one other sister and his brother-in-law were all teachers. As such, they were held in high esteem within the community. The Blair name was also Scottish in origin. John's great-grandfather, James Blair, was another adventurer who had come to Jamaica from Ayr in the late 1700s with hardly a penny to his name. He became an overseer on a Jamaican estate when he was barely in his teens and eventually came to own Hopeton Estate in south St. Elizabeth, along with twenty-seven slaves and a similar number of cows.

The great-grandson of John Blair of Dunskey, himself descended from a Norman knight named William deBlare, James Blair's Scots family was proud of its lineage. James would now do his best to extend the bloodline across the Colony by impregnating three 13-year-old slave girls in quick succession and bearing at least eleven and possibly sixteen children by them. One of these coloured children became John Blair's grandmother. To James Blair's credit, he voluntarily had eleven of his children baptized and he brought them all to Hopeton Estate to live with him, leaving his assets to them in his Will. James Blair died in 1835, just one year after the abolition of slavery by the British Parliament. Perhaps he wanted to ensure that his progeny had the best possible start under this new world order.

This is the hidden reality of slavery – not only whips and cries of pain, but also abuse of another kind committed in silence within the great estate houses, while surly male slaves worked in the fields, fearing for their sisters and daughters, in all likelihood beside themselves with anger. Slavery, then, was not merely a system of labour that enriched the estate owners and the Crown; it was equally important as a system of sexual gratification. The entire character of colonial society and the nature of the slave market, as a place of assignation as much as a place of business, changes in our perceptions as we come to understand these unreported facts.

Even today, school books used in England and Wales explicitly make the claim that contact between master and slave was very limited. This is nothing less than a falsehood, but how to tell the truth to a class filled with children of all races, many of them the descendants of the abused and others of the abusers? As we have seen, the contact was, in actuality, not merely close but exceedingly intimate.

It was as witnesses to this abuse that the final generation of soon-to-be-liberated slaves grew up, and with these memories of exploitation that they then raised their own legitimate children on the Pedro Plains and elsewhere. Whether they vocalized or even fully comprehended what had happened in the recent past is unclear, but it all added layers of complexity to social relations and to our story, for the position taken by the British Colonial Office on the recruitment of Caribbean aircrew, of which more shortly, must surely have been consciously or subconsciously influenced by a collective awareness of this history. Indeed, by 1800 there were reported to be over 10,000 'free people of colour' living in Jamaica alone and some members of this community actively supported the Crown in suppressing major slave revolts on the island. Others, most notably George William Gordon, were implicated as organizers of protests against continuing harsh conditions post-slavery and Gordon was hanged – by Royal decree – for his alleged, but unproven, part in the Morant Bay Rebellion of 1865.

The attitudes of the peoples of the Caribbean towards their colonial rulers were coloured by this past and the willingness with which so many volunteered to serve can seem paradoxical. However, there was genuine fear in the region when Nazi Germany began its period of conquest. Few people looked forward to a day when Nazi overlords would replace British ones.

Chapter 2

I Could Never Stand a Bully

The Caribbean RAF volunteers, whatever their hue, were rightly proud of their hard won freedoms, limited as those might be. When, on 1 September 1939, Nazi Germany, led by its Fuhrer Adolf Hitler, invaded Poland using the pretext that Polish terrorists had attacked a German radio station, many in the Caribbean sat up and took notice, for a Nazi victory in Europe had very serious ramifications for British colonial subjects.

The British government announced the lifting of the military colour bar on 19 October 1939, eight weeks after the start of hostilities. Up until this time the official British policy was that only 'British born men, of British born parents, of pure European descent' could receive officer's commissions in any of His Majesty's armed services. The lifting of the ban allowed British colonial subjects to volunteer for enlistment and to officially receive commissions as officers in the armed services for the first time in history.

Nevertheless, for the first six months of 1940, black volunteers were still being turned away at many British military recruiting offices, as it took time for the new rules to be communicated and even longer for them to be enforced. None of the services appeared particularly keen on accepting black candidates for any roles, regardless of what the new official policy might be. The RAF, for example, was still agitating in December 1939 for all black candidates to be steered towards the Army, which in their books was more deserving.

Then, in the wake of the Battle of Britain which had ended in the autumn of 1940, the matter of black volunteers for the RAF was re-examined. The RAF had suffered heavy losses during the battle, while black volunteers had continued to push themselves forward insistently, both in West Africa and in the West Indies. Apparently under pressure from the Colonial Office, the

RAF now relented and launched a belated recruitment drive across the black dominions, with a particular focus on the West Indies. It was as a result of this change of heart within one service that the Royal Air Force would become a haven for black officer candidates, the Army and Navy failing to follow suit.

John Ebanks was a very religious young man and even in old age he could not clearly explain his motivations for going to war. In addition to being a teacher, he was the youngest lay preacher in the Anglican Church in Jamaica. But John was very annoyed when he listened to the news and heard how Hitler was 'bulldozing his way' through smaller countries such as Poland and Czechoslovakia. As he later expressed it:

'Hitler was just a dammed bully using his strength to dominate those people.'

In early June 1940, John Ebanks was sitting with his headmistress listening to the staffroom radio when suddenly the recently appointed British Prime Minister, Winston Churchill, came on the air and they both heard that amazing speech, 'We shall fight on the beaches'. The pair were deeply moved. The Germans were rampaging across Europe and the British people, alone on their island, were going to stop them. It was this that finally triggered his decision to volunteer for the RAF. John Ebanks just could not stand a bully and he knew that the British would need all the help they could get.

Churchill's speech inspired millions of people around the world and, although it is oft quoted, I think it is worth repeating the most famous section here:

'Even though large tracts of Europe and many old and famous states have fallen, or may fall into the grip of the Gestapo and all the odious apparatus of Nazi rule, we shall not flag or fail. We shall go on to the end. We shall fight in France, we shall fight on the seas and oceans, we shall fight with growing confidence and growing strength in the air, we shall defend our island, whatever the cost may be. We shall fight on the beaches, we shall fight on the landing grounds, we shall fight in the fields and in the streets, we shall fight in the hills; we shall never surrender. And if, which I do not for a moment believe, this island or a large part of it were subjugated and starving, then our Empire beyond the seas, armed and guarded by the British Fleet, would carry on the struggle, until, in God's good time, the New World, with all its power and might, steps forth to the rescue and the liberation of the old.'

This speech was delivered by Winston Churchill to the House of Commons of the Parliament of the United Kingdom on 4 June 1940.

We must not forget that Churchill, for all his wartime successes as a motivational leader of the British people, was also an arch imperialist and that his commitment to the rights and liberties of the darker skinned peoples of the earth was at best inconsistent. Present at the Battle of Omdurman in 1898, where he rode with the 21st Lancers, Churchill was critical of Lord Kitchener's cold-blooded execution of large numbers of wounded Sudanese rebels, but this sentimentality was uncharacteristic of the man. Richard Toye in his 2010 work *Churchill's Empire*, quotes Churchill as saying that he had taken part in 'a lot of jolly little wars against barbarous peoples.' Of his operations against jihadists in the Swat Valley in what is now Pakistan, Churchill wrote, 'We proceeded systematically, village by village, and we destroyed the houses, filled up the wells, blew down the towers, cut down the shady trees, burned the crops and broke the reservoirs in punitive devastation.'

Following his election to Parliament in 1900, Churchill called for a rolling tide of British conquests around the globe, saying that 'The Aryan stock is bound to triumph'. Some of the first concentration camps ever constructed were built in South Africa by the British Army during the Boer War, and Churchill, who was present as a journalist, defended the system, claiming that the camps were responsible for 'the minimum of suffering'. This was in spite of the fact that over ten per cent of the 115,000 men, women and children so interred would perish in the camp network. Later, now in high office, he unleashed the notorious 'Black and Tans' on Ireland's catholics, in an orgy of home burnings, beatings and killings. In response to a Kurdish rebellion against British rule in Iraq, Churchill has been widely reported as having advocated the use of poison gas. What he actually said was:

'I do not understand this squeamishness about the use of gas. We have definitely adopted the position at the Peace Conference of arguing in favour of the retention of gas as a permanent method of warfare. It is sheer affectation to lacerate a man with the poisonous fragment of a bursting shell and to boggle at making his eyes water by means of lachrymatory gas. I am strongly in favour of using poisoned gas against uncivilized tribes. The moral effect should be so good that the loss of life should be reduced to a minimum. It is not necessary to use only the most deadly gasses: gasses can be used which cause great inconvenience and would spread a lively terror and yet would leave no serious permanent effects on most of those affected.'

Arguments continue today as to whether or not the RAF did in fact drop gas on the Kurds in the 1920s and exactly what type of gas that might have been. Some claim that only tear gas was used and this is indeed the common name for the 'lachrymatory gas' proposed by Churchill. His confusion between tear gas and poisoned gas was unfortunate and leaves his true intentions open to interpretation.

All the same, it was this same Churchill who recognized the threat posed by Hitler and the Nazis, years before anyone else of his stature. He spoke out bravely against the policy of appeasement at great personal and professional cost, condemning himself to a long period in political isolation. Whatever he thought of the peoples of the Empire, his insistence on trumpeting the danger in Europe and his commitment to that struggle once it began would prove central to the ultimate Allied victory. This, in turn, heralded an unintended but very real new dawn for subjugated peoples almost everywhere in a rolling tide, not of imperialism but of democratization, that continues to the present day.

When the June 1940 speech was given, 22-year-old Harry McCalla, resident of Half Way Tree, was working as a clerk in the Collector General's Department of the Revenue Services in Kingston. A career in the Royal Air Force seemed like a glamorous and exciting prospect to him and although his mother objected, his father supported the young man's ambitions, thinking that such a move would make a man of him. And so it did. Harry described the experience of leaving Jamaica for England as, 'Going from a small world into a big world... It had a revolutionary effect on my life.' Described as 'amusingly cynical, but also sensitive and touchy', Harry would first train in Canada before becoming a popular member of his Bomber Command Lancaster crew.

The day after Churchill's speech, John Ebanks went to the British military base at Up Park Camp in Kingston, where Tom Forsyth was then part of the Military Police unit on duty at the two gates of the base; 'Cotton Tree' Gate in the west and 'Duppy' Gate in the east:

> 'A very wicked officer, named Colonel Bush was once in command (here) and he had a reputation for cruelty. When he died, his body was chained in the tomb, but that could not hold his spirit. His ghost walked in the dead of night in the guise of the orderly officer and turned out the guard. Next morning, the men who had responded to the spectre's summons would be found unconscious; some never regained consciousness and those that did were never normal again. The grave of the colonel was once marked by a brick monument, but this was torn down when the Jamaica Infantry Volunteers Club was built. To this day, the vicinity is known as Bush Guard and the gate nearby as The Duppy Gate. Duppy is the Jamaican word for ghost.'

Up Park Camp remains today very much as it was in 1940. The British-built barrack rooms, surprisingly cool with their thick brick walls and large open windows, now house the infantry and engineers of the Jamaica Defence Force, but those men parade on the same parade square as the long departed colonial troops. The same chapel and guardhouse, headquarters buildings and storerooms continue to deliver the same services, but the uniforms have changed. American combat fatigues and modern helmets have replaced khaki and leather, while assault rifles have taken the place of the wood and steel of the .303 rifle and the Bren gun.

In early 1940, John Ebanks navigated his way past the stern-faced and very visible Canadian MPs and their invisible Duppy, and submitted his application to join the RAF. Then he went back to school and waited. He waited until the middle of 1941, when, more than a year after applying, he finally received orders to report for medical and mental tests. In Ebanks' view, the educational tests administered in Jamaica were much more challenging than the ones he and his colleagues later received once they arrived in England, presumably in order to ensure that any black candidates selected were demonstrably of the highest calibre and to shield them, and their selectors, from subsequent criticizm.

Following the tests, each candidate faced a series of interviews by the selection committee. The conditions of acceptance were very strict because everyone who applied for the RAF was applying for aircrew duties – no one was interested in doing anything else. John Ebanks:

'My first choice was to be a pilot but I rather foolishly achieved a 100 per cent score in the mathematics part of the test and I was told that I would probably become a navigator. I wasn't too disappointed as I knew that this was also a critical job and that many aircraft were lost not as a result of enemy fire, but due to errors in navigation.'

It was quite common at that time to hear of planes going off course and flying into mountains or heading far out to sea never to return. As a case in point, Tom Forsyth's diary shows that his unit was required to provide the burial party for an RAF pilot killed in Jamaica at the end of December 1940, so there can be little question that the volunteers were fully aware of the dangers they would face. It was not ignorance that drove them onward.

By the time John Blair had reached the age of seventeen he also decided to become a teacher and in 1938, like many of his siblings, he applied to the highly regarded Mico Teacher Training College in Kingston. Mico was founded in 1835 through the Lady Mico Charity, one of four teacher training institutions established during this period in the British colonies and the only one to survive to the present day. As a result the institution, still going strong as The Mico University College, is now the oldest teacher training institution in the Caribbean, producing one of Jamaica's most successful export products, first rate teachers. Tom Forsyth was based within walking distance of the college which boasted playing fields and a fine Victorian main building set in large grounds:

'This afternoon I saw polo being played on the polo field, and not far off, some Jamaican girls in their school uniforms were playing ground hockey with a rubber ball instead of a puck. A very stern governess chaperone disapproved of my innocent observation of her charges. I said, "This is my beat."

She retorted, "Then beat it!"'

There were other interactions between the Colonial troops and the people of the less salubrious parts of downtown Kingston:

'I had to go on duty again as traffic cop at seven outside the gate, as there is a big dance for all ranks (who are not on duty), in the NAAFI. A couple of big tents are also up for refreshment booths. Dick Wilson was the first person ejected from the dance and lodged in the guardhouse. About fifteen sailors came whose ship had just docked and they picked up some wild companions on the way to Up Park camp, all classes and colours.

'When the dance broke up, the motley crew streamed past us through the main gate and poured over the drive outside, awaiting taxis. It was three when I started to get into bed and Bob Grace came in and told me the happiest hours of his life had been spent on this island. He was so elated I could not bring myself to spoil his mood, but I thought grimly to myself, "I wish I could say that..."

'We are kidding Dick Wilson about having a dusky girlfriend. Actually she has a good education, her family are wealthy, but her father hates the military. He uses a phrase coined during the Napoleonic wars, "The brutal and licentious soldiery". Dick took her out to an expensive restaurant once; he had to "slap her hands to make her behave".

'"And who was there to slap yours?" asked Hardisty. Dick Wilson cannot go near her house if her father's home...'

The local component of the 'motley crew' represented one facet of the culture of downtown Kingston, but not all contact between Jamaicans and colonials was hedonistic. It is interesting to observe how easily education and money could overcome racial barriers. Several conventional romantic relationships developed and at least one Canadian officer married his upper middle class Jamaican girlfriend:

> 'Lieutenant (Bucky) Walker was married today to Marie DuQuesnay in a Catholic Church. Walker gave in to that, as he said her religion meant more to her than his meant to him. He is getting seven days leave for a honeymoon up in the Hills.'

The DuQuesnay family is still prominent in Jamaica and although they are Jamaicans of a lighter hue, it seems clear that relationships between white and black, rich and poor, governor and governed were more nuanced than one might assume. This would have been less true the higher one looked in colonial society, with the upper echelons of those living ex-patria remaining aloof, even from their lower caste compatriots.

In the 1930s, Mico College was already a place that many Jamaicans aspired to attend and competition for places was therefore intense, but John Blair was successful in his application and he spent three years at the College, experiencing life in the big city for the first time. In due course, John qualified as an elementary school teacher and he then joined the Greenwich School near Tinson Pen, Kingston and close to the harbour, where he taught for a year and a half.

By now, with Poland already conquered, along with Denmark and Norway in their turn, France and the Low Countries had also fallen to the Nazi regime. The Italians were fighting the British in North Africa, soon to be joined by the German Africa Korps under General Erwin Rommel, and Hitler was turning his baleful gaze towards Yugoslavia, Greece and Crete. These targets would secure Germany's southern flank in preparation for what had always been his main objective – the invasion and conquest of the Soviet Union.

The attitudes of people in the Caribbean to these developments were complex and varied. On the one hand, Tom Forsyth and his Canadian comrades were fearful of a revolt, or at least a major protest against the colonial government, potentially instigated by Alexander Bustamante, the leading trade union activist who would later become Jamaica's first elected

Prime Minister. Forsyth was helping to guard Bustamante, who was interred in Kingston along with a number of Axis prisoners of war and civilian detainees:

> 'Our job was to simply guard a camp which contained (by the time we left) over a thousand Germans and Italians and some notorious local characters, including Bustamante, who has lately caused such an uproar in the island's labour situation.
>
> 'I am one of forty men detailed to stand guard at the internment camp. The Germans have a wonderful time inside, they play football all afternoon. If they need dental care, they are taken downtown to Kingston, to a good dentist. They receive mail and parcels from Germany, they are never cold here, if it's too hot, they can sit in the shade or stay in their huts.'

But Forsyth describes the scene when a batch of captured German U-boat crewmen had to be escorted from a British ship in Kingston Harbour to the camp:

> 'For the first ten blocks, the road was lined with the (local) population, who were howling and screaming like fiends, and I couldn't help but feel we had more in common with the prisoners than with the mob outside.'

The section of downtown Kingston through which the prisoners had to pass was not representative of the Caribbean in general, it being a particularly tough and impoverished urban setting:

> 'One of our men was attacked in the Bottle Bar by a local with a pistol and another with a knife. Suffered powder burns and a bullet crease and a gash on the left side of the body from a deflected stab. Three other Grenadiers were beaten brutally about the head with broken bottles…'

Some of the Canadian soldiers were equally capable of murder and mayhem:

'Tonight, (Canadian soldier) B. Cardinal was brought into the guardhouse. He had been AWOL (absent without leave) and when searched, he was carrying a loaded revolver, $12.00 in Canadian money, and ten pounds, five shillings in British, Jamaican and Bermuda notes. He is supposed to have married the old lady who runs the Kit Kat Bar (in downtown Kingston), and whether he rifled the bar's till immediately after the ceremony or used his gun in a hold up, no one knows for sure yet. But he will be detained on general principles as a very suspicious character.'

By this time, the whole region was suffering from shortages of supplies and imported foodstuffs as a result of a concerted German U-boat campaign which later become known as The Battle of the Caribbean:

'The local paper here, the Daily Gleaner, frequently mentions mail to the UK from Bermuda having been lost, "owing to enemy action". A cargo of Xmas mail went down among other things. When our ships guard goes out to escort vessels into the harbour, the ship's crews always make some reference to German submarines.'

The Battle of the Caribbean was an extension of the larger Battle of the Atlantic. In February 1942, the U-boat fleet launched Operation Neuland, an attack on the oil refineries of the southern Caribbean and on the tankers that took the oil across the sea to the Gulf of Mexico, or up the east coast of the United States. The first attack involved a wolf pack of five U-boats under the command of Werner Hartenstein aboard U-156. The U-boats quickly sank two oil tankers off Aruba and U-67 then entered Willemstad harbour at Curaçao and torpedoed a further three tankers, although only one was sunk, the other two being hit by duds. The American Standard Oil refinery on Aruba was shelled, as was the island of Mona, off Puerto Rico.

Another dozen tankers were then sunk by U-boats at Castries St. Lucia and in Trinidad's Gulf of Paria. A second fleet of five Italian submarines patrolled the Lesser Antilles, staying on the Atlantic side of the chain of islands, and these boats sank ten ships, including several tankers. Then in

March, the German boats sank a series of tankers in the Windward passage between Cuba and Hispaniola.

When combined with numerous Allied ships sunk off Florida and up and down the east coast, as well as an attack deep in the Gulf of Mexico, it was clear to the Allies that Operation Neuland represented a serious strategic threat to the oil supply line and that countermeasures were essential. Air and Naval forces in the Caribbean were expanded and the enemy submarine threat was eventually driven out of the Caribbean, although Allied ships continued to be sunk well into 1943, including the Dutch cargo ship *Poelau Roebiah*, off Jamaica on 7 July, sunk by U-759 under Kapitänleutnant Rudolf Friedrich. The US Destroyer *Tatnall* pursued the submarine after this sinking, but was unable to find her. Two crewmen from the Dutch ship died, while sixty-eight others, along with twenty-four armed guards and thirty-one US passengers, were rescued and taken ashore.

The *Poelau Roebiah* was Rudolf Friedrich's second ever sinking, the first having occurred only two days prior. Born on 15 June 1914, at Strehlen, Silesia, Friedrich had joined the Kriegsmarine (German Navy) in 1935, aged twenty-one. Now aged twenty-eight, U-759 was Friedrich's first, and last, command. His submarine was sunk thirty-nine days out of the U-boat base at Lorient in France, by an American anti-submarine aircraft on 29 July 1943 and the entire crew of thirty-five was lost. It was the boat's second war patrol and Kriegsmarine records list the place of death as Jamaica.

With the rise in casualties, U-boat operations in the region now shifted to the Gulf of Mexico, where no less than twenty U-boats operated, sinking fifty-six vessels as they focused on the tankers out of Texas and Louisiana. By the end of 1943, a system of armed convoys was finally introduced and from that time the number of attacks diminished significantly.

Not all sunk U-boat crewmen drowned and several were held amongst the other prisoners and detainees on the island of Jamaica. These German prisoners of war did not live a completely trouble-free life, even without the verbal abuse they received from the Jamaican citizenry:

'Hallet has the true story of how the Germans came to be hurt in the scuttling of the (German ship). The crew had scuttled her and were in rowboats rowing toward the British ship, when a ship's officer ordered the Lewis gunner to fire a burst just over their heads. The gunner's family had been killed by Nazi bombs in London and he was bitter and vindictive, so he fired right on the rowboat, killing five and wounding three. He got six months detention for it. The wounded are still in the hospital. Hallet took great pleasure in teasing the wounded German sailors (so he said).

'27 June: A riot among the (German) prisoners in the internment camp. The newspaper came in with headlines of heavy fighting between the Germans and the Russians, and one prisoner shouted, "Hurray for Russia". The rest all set on him and beat him savagely. Now, this afternoon, there was a funeral for a camp inmate and we wonder if it was for the one who was beaten.'

Although they lived far from the centre of events, the people of the region knew a great deal about what was taking place in Europe, felt its effects directly and feared the possible outcome. Jamaica's educational curriculum was set by the Colonial Government and it was the same as that studied by English children. Jamaicans were therefore more familiar with British history than they were with their own and the war with Germany had also been well publicized in newspapers, radio broadcasts and in the newsreels that preceded any showing at the local cinemas.

The general view of Hitler in the West Indies was clearly that he was a man who needed to be stopped. Although many resented colonial rule, few were confused about the difference between that and what the Nazis stood for.

A significant number of people in the black dominions appear to have felt that they were all in it together with the British, and colonial subjects across the British Empire voluntarily helped to raise money in support of the war effort. This was done in addition to the extra taxes, raw materials and food that flowed from the colonies to support the British military effort and sustain the civilian population of the British home islands.

The total donated by people in the colonies, in collections, loans and personal contributions, exceeded an amount equivalent to £6.1 billion in today's money. This was a huge sacrifice made by countries with searing levels of poverty. In several cases, the funds were used to pay for aircraft which were then assigned to squadrons whose names paid tribute to the donors. Thus Jamaica Squadron, Trinidad Squadron, Ceylon Squadron, Nigeria Squadron, and several other RAF units came into existence. So it was with the attitude that a difficult but necessary job had to be done that John Blair and his comrades joined up.

The relaxation of the centuries old framework of discrimination in the officer class explains in large part why so many of the Caribbean volunteers opted for the Royal Air Force, rather than the other armed services, where commissions were still exceedingly difficult to obtain. Nevertheless, many did serve in other roles and branches. Some 15,000 black merchant seamen, most with much lower educational standards, helped to keep the vital naval supply routes to Britain open. The majority of those men stoked coal for the engines on older, slower ships and over 5,000 of them perished at sea during the conflict, once again representing a breathtaking thirty per cent of the total and another largely ignored story of loss and suffering. There were also 520 workers from the West Indies working in munitions factories in Britain and 800 forestry workers from British Honduras (now Belize) volunteered to cut timber in Scotland. This was to be a world war not only in terms of the scope of military operations, but also in terms of the involvement of people all around the planet.

Across the Caribbean, men and women began to flock to the colours and more Jamaicans entered the fray, amongst them Dudley Thompson, a future minister of government, Arthur Wint, who would later win gold in the 100 metres at the 1948 London Olympics, and Michael Manley, a future Prime Minister of Jamaica, whose father Norman had served during the First World War. Wint's brother, John Lloyd Wint, went along and qualified as a flight engineer. Lincoln Orville Lynch joined up and became an air gunner in Halifax bombers, serving as a tail gunner with John Blair in No. 102 Squadron.

William 'Billy' Strachan of Kingston, Jamaica, left school in December 1939, only four months after war broke out. His one ambition was to join the RAF and learn to fly and he made his own way to Britain by ship. The voyage across the forbidding Atlantic took many days and there was also the threat of German U-boat attacks. The U-boat menace was already very real at this time and the German submarines were sinking large numbers of merchant vessels. Broke, and with all his belongings stuffed into a single suitcase, Strachan disembarked safely in England on a typically grey and wet Saturday in early 1940 and headed for the Air Ministry in London to offer his services.

Lilian Bader, born in Great Britain and believed to have been of either Jamaican or Barbadian parentage, became the first black woman to serve in the regular British Armed Forces, where she found important employment on the ground as an aircraft instrument repair technician. A number of other West Indian women were accepted for duty in Great Britain and 6,000 male volunteers were enlisted for a wide range of ground roles within the RAF, maintaining aircraft, radios, radars, and weapons, encoding and decoding signals like Carl Chantrielle from Jamaica, as well as performing the hazardous job of loading bombs onto aircraft.

Donald Jones, also of Jamaica, was one of the Caribbean men who joined up as RAF ground crew. Sailing from Kingston, Jones was trained at the Butlin's holiday camp in Filey, now in North Yorkshire, which had been leased to the RAF for the duration by its owner and temporarily renamed RAF Hunmanby Moor. Along with two other sites in Ayr, birthplace of John Blair's great-grandfather, and Pwllheli, Filey was extensively expanded and improved by the RAF before being handed back, free of charge, to the business savvy Butlin when the war ended.

Four thousand West Indian ground crew volunteers trained at Filey and the camp features in Andrea Levy's book *Small Island*, which tells the story of these men. Unfortunately, the BBC film of the book was set elsewhere and local memory of the West Indian contingent at Filey has largely faded away. They receive no mention of any kind in the local museum, unique though their presence was. Jones spent the war working at various RAF bases in Great Britain, returning to his homeland after the war to raise a family and his daughter later became this writer's sister-in-law.

Another Jamaican member of RAF ground crew was Claude Campbell, originally from Meyersville, in St. Elizabeth, but having spent all of his youth in Catadupa, St. James. Joining the RAF in 1944, he served as a vehicle mechanic with 247 Maintenance Unit, RAF Bicester, in Oxfordshire. Campbell later recalled the preparations on the morning of 6 June 1946, for a parade of the RAF West Indian contingent before His Majesty King

George VI and Queen Elizabeth, at which Princess Elizabeth (now Queen Elizabeth II) was also present.

Campbell explains that two hundred British West Indian officers and other ranks were selected from various RAF stations to travel to London for this parade. During the inspection, Campbell claims that the Queen only stopped once and that she spoke directly to him, asking him his name, RAF station and which country he was from. Ignoring his sergeant major's instructions to say nothing more than 'Yes ma'am', or 'No ma'am', in response to any question, whatever its nature, Campbell looked the Queen in the eye and engaged her in a short discussion. Speaking in 2013, Campbell laughed and claimed that the Queen had picked him out from all the others because he was the most handsome airman in the front rank. After the parade he was accused by his mates of trying to charm the Queen, as he had a reputation as a bit of a womanizer. A photo of the occasion, included in the plates, seems to support Campbell's claim. He is standing, second from right in the image, and the Queen does appear to have spotted him. Campbell stayed in the RAF until February 1948 and was awarded the Victory Medal and the Defence Medal.

Carl Chantrielle joined up in 1943 and travelled to Filey as part of a contingent of 2,000 volunteers. He was to be trained as an encoder in an RAF Signals Unit. During the voyage from Kingston the men were fed split pea soup, after which they encountered a violent storm. Chantrielle says that having once witnessed the results of split pea induced seasickness, simultaneously afflicting hundreds of men in a confined space, he has never again been able to touch that particular soup.

Off the coast of Ireland the volunteers came on deck to watch their escort vessels depth charging a German submarine that had attempted to attack the convoy in which they were sailing. Huge spouts of seawater towered above them from the explosions, cascading down and soaking the onlookers. A dead whale floated to the surface, ripped apart from the force of the blasts.

Once at his operational base, Chantrielle recalls that he witnessed an angry encounter between a Trinidadian fighter pilot and a British Military Police corporal. The pilot was walking around camp wearing slippers with his uniform – a serious offence in the eyes of the MPs – when he was accosted by the corporal. Rounding on his accuser, the pilot, who was of Chinese extraction, said in a strong Trinidadian accent, 'Listen, it was a fight I was looking when I came here, right? So, if you want a fight it's me you want!' The corporal gave up and left the young flyer alone.

In 2013, Carl Chantrielle was entering the UK at Heathrow Airport and found himself standing in a long line of non-EU entrants. While he stood there waiting, he saw a group of German travellers passing quickly through the EU passports line and he thought to himself that things had not turned out quite as he expected; he had defended Britain against those people, but now they are welcomed, while he is treated as a foreigner.

Barbados, an island of a mere 166 square miles with a 1940 population of 179,000, sent two early contingents of recruits to join the Allied war effort. The first contingent sailed from the island on the 27 July 1940 and was recruited for the armed forces in general. The second contingent was recruited specifically for the RAF and departed Barbados in November 1940, in the immediate aftermath of the Battle of Britain. The twelve men selected for this batch included one Errol W. Barrow, who would survive the war, enter politics and eventually become the first Prime Minister of independent Barbados, between 1966 and 1976.

The easternmost of the islands of the Lesser Antilles and sometimes accused of truly being in the Atlantic rather than the Caribbean, Barbados was first visited by Spanish explorers in the early 1500s, appearing on a Spanish map in 1511. The fate of its indigenous Amerindian people was the same as that of most of the original islanders in the region, either taking flight, becoming captives, or being slain by the invaders or by their diseases. Soon none remained. Other indigenous peoples in the region who did survive claim that the original name for Barbados was 'Ichirouganaim', thought to mean 'Redstone island with teeth outside', a reference to the island's reefs.

Portuguese explorers quickly introduced wild pigs to serve as a future source of fresh meat for passing ships, but the Portuguese did not settle the island and it remained unclaimed by any of the European powers until the arrival of an English ship, the *Olive Blossom*, in 1624. Barbados thus became an early English colony within the dominions of King James I and the first settlers arrived from England in 1627, followed shortly after by the African slaves who would cultivate their sugar plantations for the next two centuries. Barbados remained a British possession until independence in 1966, giving it the distinction of being the only Caribbean island not to change colonial hands during its history.

The roll call of the second Barbadian RAF contingent is indicative of the heavy price that the West Indies would pay during the war, with exactly half of the volunteers from this batch meeting their deaths in action:

- Errol W. Barrow
- G. A. Barrow
- Mark R. Cuke   – Killed in action
- Grey D. Cumberbatch   – Killed in action
- Andrew P. C. Dunlop   – Killed in action
- Charles P. King   – Killed in action
- Bruce F. H. Miller   – Killed in action
- J. S. Partridge
- Arthur A. W. Walrond   – Killed in action
- Arthur O. Weeks
- H. E. S. Worme
- J. L. L. Yearwood

A group photo taken on their departure from the island reveals that about half the contingent was black or coloured and the remainder were white Barbadians.

Many Trinidadians also volunteered, amongst them Pilot Officer Collins A. Joseph, the son of one Elmie Joseph of San Fernando, Trinidad, who, like Arthur Weeks from Barbados and several other black or coloured volunteers, would become a Spitfire pilot and fly over Europe.

Officially Spanish until 1797, but primarily settled by French colonists, Trinidad was incorporated into a single crown colony with the nearby island of Tobago in 1888. First settled by the Archaic peoples of South America, human settlement on Trinidad has been dated at 7,000 years. Close to the coast of Venezuela, Trinidad was a stepping stone for successive waves of Amerindian tribes that moved on up the chain of Caribbean islands over many centuries, reaching as far as Cuba and Jamaica. By 1940, the island's proximity to the Venezuelan oilfields had made it another point of strategic importance and a large RAF base was situated there.

One dashing Trinidadian Spitfire pilot was Flight Sergeant James Hyde of San Juan, and others included Gilbert Huber and Winston Racy. Mervyn Cipriani would fly in Bomber Command and be killed over the German city of Kassell, while Kenrick Rawlins eventually became a bomber pilot, but was killed on his seventh mission. Pilot Officer W.E. Recile from the island flew Spitfires over Europe during 1944 and 1945.

Without question, the most illustrious Trinidadian volunteer, and one of the most successful Caribbean RAF airman overall, was Ulric Cross. Born in 1917 and therefore 22-years-old when the war broke out, Cross did his initial military training at the RAF station at Piarco in Trinidad and then, like many of the other trainees, he waited for over six months to hear what his fate might be:

'After high school at St. Mary's Port of Spain, I worked for a while with the Trinidad government on the railroad. But by 1941, Britain stood alone. Dunkirk had been a defeat for Britain and Hitler had conquered all of Europe. The world was drowning in fascism and America was not yet in the war, so I decided to do something about it and volunteered to fight in the RAF. We took the ship (*Strathallan*) for twelve days, straight to Greenock (in Scotland). A lorry awaited us and took us straight into the uniform of the RAF and training.'

E. R. Braithwaite, author of the successful autobiographical novel, *To Sir, With Love*, published in 1959 and later made into a film in 1967, joined the RAF from British Guyana as a fighter pilot and served with distinction. Leo Balderamos joined up from British Honduras.

At least three Cuban RAF volunteers flew during the conflict. Sergeant Ricardo Losa, an air gunner, served with 49 Squadron Bomber Command. He was killed along with his entire crew en-route to Berlin on 16 December 1943 and I am writing this sentence on the seventieth anniversary of his death. It was his first combat operation. On that one night, twenty-five Lancaster bombers were shot down and another thirty-two were lost due to accidents. Canadian Tom Forsyth had some contact with Cubans in Jamaica when they came to play softball against the Canadian troops:

'The Cubans were talking exclusively in Spanish, jabbering away at a great rate. One of our men was up to bat and had one strike on him. He turned to the catcher and said, "Why can't you talk a white man's language?"

'At the same time, the pitcher shot a straight fast one across the plate and the catcher remarked, in perfect English, "That's two on you, brother!"'

The smallest of the Caribbean islands also offered up many of their sons. J. R. Henry of Antigua and Osmund Alleyne of Dominica both trained together as wireless operator/air gunners before joining operational squadrons. In Alleyne's case, he would serve in North Africa and the Mediterranean, supporting the Allied invasion of Sicily.

Flight engineer Basil Johnson joined from the Bahamas. After being rejected three times he finally succeeded in gaining entry and he served initially with 114 Squadron Bomber Command and later with the elite Pathfinder Force of Group 8, where he flew with 156 Squadron. Osmond Kelsick from Montserrat served as a Typhoon pilot with 175 Squadron.

Meanwhile, small numbers of black volunteers were also arriving in Great Britain from West Africa. Johnny Smythe was born in June 1915, in Freetown, capital of Sierra Leone. Before the war, he joined the Freetown City Council and became a sub-inspector of plant and produce for the Agricultural Department. In 1939, Smythe enlisted in the colony's Local Defence Corps, reaching the rank of sergeant. Having been sponsored by the Sierra Leone Government, he then volunteered for the RAF and after training for a year he successfully qualified as a Bomber Command navigator. Smythe said later that he joined up because of his hatred of Hitler's extreme racist policies, citing Hitler's alleged refusal to shake the hand of the black champion sprinter from the USA, Jesse Owens, at the 1936 Berlin Olympic Games. Smythe was the only volunteer out of a group of ninety from Sierra Leone to successfully complete the selection and training processes and qualify for RAF operations, although he was followed later by Adesanya Hyde, who became a flight sergeant and a navigator in Halifax bombers, winning a DFC for his 'tenacity and unfailing devotion to duty' in the process and surviving the war.

Sierra Leone has an even stronger link to the Caribbean than the rest of West Africa. After its defeat in the American War of Independence, the British Government decided to relocate a large number of freed slaves from a failed settlement in Nova Scotia to Sierra Leone, where it was felt they would be more at home and more likely to prosper. Only a very small number of these 'returning' former slaves had ever set foot in Africa. Most members of the group were escapees from American plantations who had heeded an offer from the British; their freedom in return for their escape. This was a British stratagem designed to undermine the economy of the rebellious colonies of North America. But the group also included a number of Jamaican Maroons who had been banished from the island after the Second Maroon War in the 1790s. Many of these returnees kept their anglicized slave names and these can still be found in Sierra Leone.

Despite West Africa's historical ties to the black peoples of the Caribbean, the West African recruitment drive would fail to achieve the success of its Caribbean counterpart. At this time, not only the clubs and hotels, but even the passageways within the British military headquarters in Lagos were still racially segregated, with one set of passageways being reserved for whites and another for blacks. By this means it was ensured that no white man need pass too close to a black man in the same building. Racial segregation in Africa had a sharper edge than the policies being applied in the Caribbean and it is difficult to imagine the kinds of interaction between blacks and whites that occurred regularly and openly in the islands taking place on the African continent, although some crossover did of course occur.

The RAF had launched its recruitment drive in the West Indies very early in the war, but as it viewed West Africa through a different lens, it would take continued pressure by those Africans wishing to serve before the policy of discrimination would be revised there. One such would-be volunteer was Peter 'Deniyi' Thomas, son of one of Nigeria's wealthiest and most influential men, Mr J. C. Thomas.

Peter Thomas was well educated, athletic and a serving member of the Nigerian Regiment. His father, a prominent Nigerian, is said to have donated several Spitfires to the RAF and with the active support of Charles Woolley, the Colonial Chief Secretary to the Nigerian government, Peter became the first black West African to qualify as a pilot and the first to receive an officer's commission in any of His Majesty's Forces, serving as a pilot officer in Britain as early as 1941. Peter Thomas was killed late in the war, in January 1945, when the aircraft he was piloting crashed during a training flight.

In spite of this individual breakthrough, with its tragic outcome, the results of the Air Ministry's March 1941 West African recruitment drive were disappointing. In Nigeria for example, 500 applications were received, of which 271 were considered by the Selection Board. Forty-eight candidates were passed by the board, but all of these later failed on medical grounds, because one key requirement of the RAF tests was that a candidate must have been free of malaria for a continuous period of six months, irrespective of race or origin.

Similar challenges were experienced in the Gold Coast, where only four volunteers were accepted from a total of fifty-eight, and in Gambia, where only one volunteer could be found who met the requisite educational and medical standards. The Royal Air Force pointed out forcefully that recruitment standards were being applied uniformly around the Empire and that in the West Indies several thousand black and coloured candidates for various roles had been accepted and passed as medically fit. The RAF denied that there was any racial element to its failure to find substantial numbers of West African volunteers. However, some commentators have suggested that the British recruitment policy in West Africa was influenced by fears about the ways in which advanced military skills might be put to use to support local independence struggles post-war. As always, the truth may sit somewhere in the middle.

Tom Forsyth, while ignorant of the RAF's particular challenges, sheds some light on the differences between the colonial experience of service in West Africa and service in the West Indies when he describes an encounter with a unit of British troops arriving in Jamaica following a one year stint in Sierra Leone:

'They came from Sierra Leone, "The white man's grave"; they had all had malaria, had been a month on the water and were still convalescing from the fever. They had been on the Dark Continent for five months. No troops were ever allowed to stay in that location for more than a year and a half... They say this is heaven compared to Sierra Leone. The Essex moved into Freetown, Sierra Leone a thousand strong. They have had as many as 500 in the hospital at one time with malaria. Four men died the first month they were there.'

Small groups of West African RAF recruits did make the journey to Britain over the coming years, including David Oguntoye, an elementary school supervisor from Lagos who arrived in 1943, and Bankole Oki. A few months later, V. A. Roberts, N. Akinbehin and Godfrey Petgrave arrived in Liverpool by ship, having been subjected to enemy air attack on route. But whether you regard him as lucky or unlucky, by the time David Oguntoye had completed his training in Canada and Britain, the war had ended.

Oguntoye was undeniably lucky in love, if not in war. During his service in England he met and married a Kentish girl who later returned to Nigeria with him, becoming in due course Dulcie Ethel Adunola Oguntoye, High Court Justice, Tribal Chief and published author. Encouraged by her husband, she had enrolled for law at the Middle Temple Inns of Court shortly after the end of the conflict. Totally commited to Nigeria, Justice Oguntoye, whose husband has now passed away, continues to live in Nigeria where she is still an active commentator on current affairs.

Robert Nbaronje stowed away in the coal bunker of an English ship in order to make the journey from Nigeria to Great Britain. After ten days of hunger and thirst he gave himself up and was immediately put to work painting and shovelling coal. Once he finally arrived in England he successfully applied to join the RAF.

Another West African member of Bomber Command aircrew was Flight Sergeant Akin Shenbanjo, a navigator who had enlisted in 1941, presumably in England. Shenbanjo had the unusual honour of having his aircraft unofficially named after him by the rest of the crew and ground staff. Halifax LW648, 'The Black Prince', also had the German word 'Achtung!' placed ahead of the name painted on its nose – Achtung, the Black Prince cometh!

In total, it appears that no more than about fifty West African aircrew served operationally in the RAF during the war. At the same time, as many as half a million West Africans served on the ground with British and French forces, making a massive contribution to the war efforts of both nations. More than 75,000 black African soldiers were serving in France at the time of the German invasion in 1940, and of these an estimated 10,000 were killed during the debacle. The men were enlisted primarily from the French colonies of Niger, Senegal and Mauritania and the Tirailleurs Sénégalais were reportedly singled out for harsh treatment by the soldiers of the Wehrmacht, in part because of the Tirailleurs' use of the 'coupes-coupes' (machetes) as a combat weapon. At least 1,500 Tirailleurs were executed by the Germans in cold blood after capture, possibly as many as 3,000, but many thousands of other African PoWs were sent unharmed to Germany where they were used throughout the war as slave labour. Other forgotten black units include the men of the 81st and 82nd (West Africa) Divisions, both of which served with distinction as part of the British Fourteenth Army, helping to fight the Japanese to a standstill in Burma near Kohima and throughout the Arakan campaign of 1944.

In a form of reverse racism, the British authorities in India are said to have helped to spread rumours that the arriving African soldiers were all cannibals and that they had tails – in order to talk up their combat potential. This terrified Indian and Japanese alike, and the men later reported that they were asked to keep their boxer shorts on when bathing in order that their 'tails' not offend the local populace. The West Africans were more at home in the Burmese jungle than either the British or Japanese and this gave them a significant advantage. As for the Japanese, the sight of hundreds of West African 'cannibals' approaching through the trees and menacingly brandishing machetes was perhaps sometimes enough to send them packing.

I trained in India myself as an officer candidate seconded to the Indian Military Academy from the Jamaica Defence Force in the late 1970s. One of my fellow students, Locksley Thomas, was a very tall Jamaican of dark complexion and the Academy's heavyweight boxing champion. Whenever we passed through the rural Indian villages on manoeuvres, dozens of children would come out of their huts to see Locksley passing, touching him warily on the arms and crying out the Hindu words for 'Black Demon'! However, I never heard them ask about his tail.

In spite of the odds against them and the dangers before them, the black RAF volunteers made their way to the battle, singly or in small groups, by ship across vast expanses of ocean infested by German U-boats. They travelled from the sunshine and warmth of the tropics to the strangeness of their cold, damp training bases in Britain and Canada. Few had ever left their own shores before, none had ever flown in an aircraft, and until the outbreak of war not a man had dared hope that he would one day become a British military aviator.

Chapter 3

Piss Off!; Cold as the Devil; Black Fighter Boys

D espite the lifting of the colour bar and the launch of the recruitment drives across the Empire's black dominions, many men and women who wished to volunteer their services to Britain's fighting forces still faced unofficial barriers to entry and not all West Indians found joining the RAF an easy process. When Billy Strachan arrived in England from Jamaica in early 1940, still travelling under his own steam, he made his way to Adastral House in London, the home of the Air Ministry throughout the Second World War. Arriving at the main entrance, he spoke to the RAF corporal at the door:

> 'I said to him, "I'd like to join the Air Force". "He said to me, I'll never forget this, he said, "Piss off".'
>
> (Imperial War Museum Collection.
> Transcript of interview with William Strachan.)

Strachan was not deterred by this initial rebuff. After all, he had just voyaged halfway across the globe in wartime to volunteer, so a few rude corporals were not going to stop him now. He eventually succeeded in submitting his application and gaining acceptance as an RAF aircrew trainee. After twelve weeks of basic military training, Strachan was then sent on a wireless operator/air gunner course in preparation for Bomber Command operations.

Only a year before the formal lifting of the bar, Cy Grant's close friend, Sydney Kennard, had applied to the RAF but been refused entry. Kennard was the coloured son of an English doctor and his black wife. He already possessed a pilot's licence, obtained in the USA, and he had paid his own way to England for the purpose of joining up. But the RAF had not yet suffered the 3,000 casualties of the Battle of France and the Battle of

Britain, and Kennard was turned away on racial grounds. Now, with pilots in desperately short supply, the doors of RAF recruiting centres were flung open wide for men of colour from the Caribbean, and a little less widely for volunteers from West Africa. Cy Grant took the tests and passed 'A1', the highest score achievable. I have been unable to find any record of a Sydney Kennard joining the RAF from the Caribbean and it appears that either his initial rebuff was sufficient to turn him away permanently, or that he volunteered to serve in some other capacity.

It is impossible to understand the mindset of black volunteers from either the Caribbean or Africa, or to comprehend the reactions of their white contemporaries, without considering their respective social and cultural frames of reference, for what we might consider exceptionally racist today was often commonplace, even unremarkable at the time. But what motivates the actions of a man who has been told since birth that he is racially inferior, yet who knows in his heart that this is not true? It is very often the desire to prove himself the equal of his supposed betters through words and deeds. And what better ways to achieve this than to become educated and to join in righteous battle alongside the colonial master? For many in the Caribbean, the Second World War was an opportunity to prove themselves the equal of their British overlords.

Few Caribbean people were familiar with the reality of white European working class life, of the slums and the stinking, dangerous, polluted factories, the tough conditions of life on the farms, or the short-lived existence of the unnaturally stunted men who worked the mines. The Caribbean volunteers had been raised on Wordsworth and Tennyson, and they could recite by heart William Blake's original short poem celebrating England's green and pleasant land. Many of the new arrivals in England had half expected to find a land of castles, cricket and village greens, populated by a cultured race of well adapted servants and congenial lords. The grimy, war battered, undernourished and often crudely vocalized reality was a shock. The volunteer's eyes stung and their noses itched from the soot and smoke of the big cities, their stomachs struggled to digest the poor wartime diet, and they shivered from the cold and damp as they tried to warm themselves in their wooden huts, huddling beside decrepit radiators decorated with other men's wet and smelly socks. Yet, as the volunteers talked wistfully of the warm sunshine and properly seasoned home cooking they had left behind, they also understood that they had done the right thing; they felt they really could help these people in their struggle.

For most, interactions with the colonial whites had been very limited. Engaging with white men now as equals, much less as subordinates, required a huge mental shift that only the most flexible and robust character could handle with aplomb and for many of the men coming to terms with the reality of a subservient, less well educated white working class was another epiphany. Arriving for training at RAF Cranwell, Billy Strachan was introduced to his first batman, a form of military manservant and a man who had once been batman to the future King George VI when he had been at the facility as Officer in Charge of Boys:

'The batman was a very smooth Jeeves type and exactly the kind
of character I had been led to expect. Meanwhile, I was just a
little coloured boy from the Caribbean. When I first met him, I
instinctively called this English batman, "Sir".

"No, Sir," the Batman hastily corrected me, "It is I who call you
Sir."'

The fact that the white British population, and in particular the exclusively white members of the RAF, were able to make this cultural shift themselves, and in the space of only two years, represents one of the most astounding social and organizational transformations in modern history. Rather than being ignored, it deserves to be studied in great detail, for within it lie lessons from which we could doubtless profit today.

Yet this acceptance by the British of the new black arrivals was in stark contrast to the attitude displayed by many of the American troops, who would soon start arriving in Britain, toward their own black servicemen. The United States of America had permitted black men to wear uniform and bear arms since the American Civil War. However, this was only allowed in segregated units led by white officers and that practice was still in force throughout the Second World War. White American troops, particularly those from the southern states, were often incensed to see the British allowing coloured servicemen from the dominions to mix freely in bars, clubs and theatres and to associate intimately with white British girls. In at least one case, a black RAF fighter pilot was beaten up and thrown out of an English pub by white American bomber crewmen on account of his race. Some dominion soldiers also reacted violently to the sight of black soldiers preparing for combat duties. There were reports of physical attacks on coloured troops by South African soldiers who were deeply upset by the sight of 'blacks with guns'.

For their own part, the Germans seem to have been unsure about how to respond to the unexpected arrival, by parachute, of black RAF officers who had been shot down. Although the precise fate of some of these men is not known and even white aircrew are known to have been lynched by German mobs, most of the black airmen who were eventually taken prisoner appear to have been reasonably well treated by their Luftwaffe captors. On the whole, the behaviour of the Luftwaffe, which ran a separate prison camp system for Allied aircrew (comprising a network of Stammlager Luftwaffe, more commonly known as the 'Stalag Luft' camps), contrasted very positively with that of the SS troops who ran the Nazi concentration camp system, or even that of the German Army which brutalized and neglected the millions of Russian prisoners it captured, leading to the deaths of over two million through starvation, beatings and shootings. It is likely that the mutual respect that has always existed between airmen of most nations, extended to cover Caribbean and West African crewmen, regardless of their colour, but it is also the case that the Nazis did not have genocidal intent towards the black races, whatever the contempt in which they may have held them.

After the war had ended it would be established that by 1944 an incredible twenty-five per cent of occupied Europe's workforce was composed of slaves, most being captured Soviet soldiers, Jewish concentration camp detainees and political prisoners, but they also included other Allied prisoners of war and large numbers of men taken by force from the occupied nations. In a strange twist of fate, the free black grandchildren of the former slave populations of Europe's colonies had now come to help secure the release of Europe's new generation of white slaves from bondage. And they had come of their own volition.

Cold as the Devil

The first thing she said was, *'I always heard coloured people couldn't fly airplanes, but I see you're flying all around here.'*
And then she said, *'I'm just going to have to take a flight with you.'*
After the flight she said, *'Well, I see you can fly all right!'*

First Lady Eleanor Roosevelt
during her visit to the Tuskegee Airmen, March 1941

Ulric Cross was lucky. The *Strathallan*, the ship assigned to take him and his fellow volunteers across the Atlantic, was a converted liner. Launched in September 1937, the last of five sister ships with the same tonnage, the vessel had first sailed for Australia where she and her crew made a few pleasure cruises around the South Pacific region before war broke out and she was requisitioned for naval service. Converted to a troopship and painted in military gray, she was nevertheless a more comfortable proposition than the cargo vessels that many recruits would have to endure. Despite the U-boat menace, the *Strathallan* sailed unescorted at maximum speed across the Atlantic to Scotland, zigzagging all the way and carrying the volunteers as well as troops from existing military units who were returning home.

John Ebanks also travelled to England by ship, but after a few months he was posted to Canada for training. This required a second Atlantic voyage, which would be followed by a third once his training was completed. John described the good time he had in Canada:

'There was no blackout, there was plenty to eat and the girls were very nice, although that didn't interest me as I was a devout Christian!'

What did disturb him was a comment that people who trained in Canada as navigators were at a disadvantage because the lack of a blackout made night navigation comparatively easy. John Ebanks and his ten Caribbean comrades described themselves as the '11/11' Club, implying that they hoped all eleven members of the group would survive the war. Only two would do so.

John Blair had also been accepted for RAF training and after returning home briefly to St. Elizabeth to bid farewell to his family, he left for

Kingston on the fish truck that ran regularly from in front of the old Pedro Plains Post Office. In those days the trip took several hours. When the truck started the long climb up the steep side of Spur Tree Hill towards the town of Mandeville in the central highlands of Jamaica, it began to overheat. To make matters worse, the brakes were so poorly maintained, due to shortages of parts, that when the driver stopped to top up the radiator the passengers had to jump down quickly and put large stones behind the rear wheels to prevent the vehicle from rolling backwards down the hill and losing its valuable cargo of fish. By the time they arrived in Kingston they all agreed that they were already in need of a holiday.

In October 1942, after a short period of orientation at Up Park Camp, about thirty Jamaican RAF aircrew volunteers left the island by ship, bound for Canada. They were off to commence their training for war. John, a 23-year-old elementary school teacher from Pedro Plains, was on his way to fly against the Nazi war machine. He was too young and naive to feel real fear and his main emotion was excitement at the prospect of seeing places and peoples he had only ever read about in books. The possibility of death or injury was far from his mind.

The volunteers were ordered to board an American ship in Kingston harbour. The U.S. crew regarded these black passengers coldly and pointed below decks, saying, 'You all go down there'. When the men descended to the next deck they saw rows of empty bunks. Everyone selected a bed and they started to make themselves at home.

They did not have time to get comfortable, because within a few minutes a white officer appeared and shouted, 'No! Not here. Go down two more levels!' And so the volunteers spent the rest of their time on the ship sitting in the hold. Educated men, willing volunteers and future fliers they might be, but for now they were just black men, to be segregated and denied access to the world inhabited by decent white folk.

Tom Forsyth met and chatted with a group of American sailors in Kingston Harbour shortly before John Blair's first contact with the type:

'They deplore the fact that the blacks here do not show any respect for white men, compared to the ones in the U.S.'

And then later:

> 'Yates brought in a U.S. Marine for supper. He was from Alabama and
> said the blacks here have never been taught properly how to respect
> white folk like in the U.S.A.'

Forsyth keeps his own opinions on the matter to himself, but reading
between the lines of his diary, I sense that these remarks left him feeling
uncomfortable.

It was at this time that John Blair's friendship with Arthur Wint became
established. Both men were keen athletes. This was John's first time on the
open sea and his first time outside Jamaica, so he felt fortunate to be in a
good group of fellows, as it banished thoughts of loneliness from his mind.
But the ship pitched and rolled heavily and it was dark, stifling and damp in
the hold. Several of the men were sick and the smell in that confined place
made the journey particularly difficult.

They were going the long way around the Caribbean rim and they docked
for a short time in British Honduras. Here they took on board some forestry
workers who had volunteered for labour duties, as well as a few more RAF
volunteers, including Leo Balderamos, with whom John quickly made
friends. John chatted with some of the forestry workers and learned that
they were going to Scotland and would be working in the forests reputed to
be found there, cutting timber.

This enlarged group now sailed together as far as New Orleans where
they disembarked with great relief, for conditions had been extremely
cramped after the newcomers were shoved below decks as well. Leaving the
forestry workers behind, the RAF party now journeyed to New York by train
and spent two weeks there waiting to be told where they should go next.
This was a chance to have a good look around, and they made full use of it.
Leo Balderamos joined John Blair on a trip to the top of the Empire State
Building, at that time the tallest structure ever built, and after a life in the
West Indies and weeks stuck in the hold of a ship, this was a real adventure.

Finally their orders arrived and they set off once again, bound for
the largest RAF station in Canada, at Moncton in New Brunswick. The
Moncton camp covered many acres and held a large number of trainees.

Almost all Royal Air Force students bound for the United Kingdom came through there at some point and whether they were destined for training in Canada or elsewhere, Moncton was the transit camp. The base was swarming with recruits.

At Moncton the men were issued with their first uniforms and given basic military training. This had nothing to do with flying but it was the initial requirement for getting into any of the armed services. A lot of the recruit's time was taken up by drill parades, with much saluting and stamping of the feet, and some of the most terrifying drill instructors were British or Irish émigrés to Canada:

'Wipe that bloody grin off your face! How tall are you? Six foot effing two? Corporal, did you hear that? Can they pile shit that high these days then? Squad shun! Slope arms! Correct that slope; YOU'RE NOT HOLDING A SPEAR NOW MY FRIEND! Order arms! Present arms! Chin in, stomach in, chest out! Wot are things coming to? You 'orrible little man – wot do you think you're looking at? Squad, by the left, quick march! Left, right, left, right, left, right, left! Squad... Halt! Right turn! Left turn! About turn! LIFT THOSE KNEES UP! Call yourself an airman? Hitler must be laughing his head off at the thought of you! I will now demonstrate the correct position. Points to note! My right thigh is protruding from my body at an angle of 90 degrees and is parallel to the ground. My toe is pointing to the front and is in line with my heel. WHO TOLD YOU TO MOVE? Give me one lap around the square! No, not running lad – frog jumps! You're not relaxing under the coconut trees now matey!' (I invented this 'quote' based on personal experience of a similar training regime.)

The men were also taught how to maintain and fire a rifle. John had never touched a gun before and he felt that he was undergoing quite an initiation. The .303 rifle weighed in at just over 8lbs and when the recruit's webbing, packs, water and ammunition were added, the basic load that they would carry on their long and exhausting route marches amounted to over 40lbs. When John Blair held the wooden stock to his cheek and pulled the trigger for the first time, the heavy rifle bucked and slammed into his cheek bone. After only a few rounds his face was bruised and sore and he promised himself that, come what may, it would be the Air Force and not the infantry for him.

The recruit's first uniforms were uncomfortable and made them itch and chafe. In addition to trousers and jacket, they had been given a heavy greatcoat and great big black leather boots, with hobnails in the soles and steel on the heels. These made a crisp sound as they marched and made them feel as though they really were soldiers now, but they also gave them blisters and left their feet painfully raw. The boots had to be prepared. First, the men lit candles and heated old spoons, using the hot metal to burn the bumps off the toecaps, creating a smooth surface ready to take a high polish. This was followed by a painstaking process of polishing and burnishing, applying surface upon surface with shoe polish, water and cotton wool until the toes gleamed like water themselves. Even the soles of the boot were polished until they shone black. The recruits could literally see their faces in their reflections, although their instructors were less than impressed by these first efforts. Buttons and buckles were burnished with Brasso, webbing was painted with Blanco, needle and thread were applied to trousers, while soap was applied to the insides of uniform creases prior to ironing, to serve as starch, and weapons were cleaned and then cleaned again. Thus, the evenings were generally spent sitting on the edges of bunk beds in their barrack rooms, cleaning their kit, and telling jokes or speculating about the future.

John Blair left Moncton at the end of November 1942, bound for the Royal Canadian Air Force training station at Crumlin, Ontario, for flight navigator training. There were now twenty-one men in total and they had become a multi-cultural bunch. Two Englishmen had joined and the group 'covered all shades from black to white and everything in-between'. One of the Englishmen was a teacher like John Blair, although this man had taught at a college in Britain. The other had been living in Belize. This band of brothers travelled and lived together without tension.

After another three weeks of classroom work they were sent to Toronto to be assessed. This ironing out phase was a critical period for anyone whose ambition was to fly. The trainees attended more lectures and they then sat exams on a variety of subjects. The results would determine once and for all which end of the airfield they were destined for, aircrew or ground staff. Those who failed to qualify for flight training were sent away to be trained for other roles. The recruits later said that this process was conducted purely on the basis of qualifications and not race. The two Englishmen were selected for preliminary flight crew training, as were Arthur Wint, Lincoln Lynch, Leo Balderamos and John Blair.

Most of those selected for aircrew were sent to McGill University, where they spent four weeks in the classroom. This phase of their training took place during the deep, dark and bitterly cold Canadian winter. This was something none of the West Indians had ever experienced and the snow was up to their knees as they walked between the buildings.

Unexpectedly, John Blair and Arthur Wint were pulled out of their classes one day and sent to a special school in Ottawa. They felt that their names had simply been pulled out of a hat and nobody had even made arrangements for their accommodation, so they had to sort that out for themselves. Eventually, it dawned on the pair that the Canadians had somehow got the idea that the men did not know anything about mathematics. When the special classes commenced, Wint and Blair realized that they were being taught the most basic levels of algebra and trigonometry. On the very first day they looked at each other and said, 'This is a joke!' Then Arthur Wint said, 'Look, let's try and show these people what we are capable of.'

The teacher came into the room for their second session and started by setting up a simple algebraic problem on the blackboard. Wint spoke up and asked him to set the men a more difficult challenge. The teacher looked at Wint for a long moment and then turned back to the blackboard and wrote up a much more complex problem. It was evident that he thought Arthur Wint was going to make a mess of it, but Wint solved the problem with ease and in quick order he and John Blair were sent to resume their training with their group at McGill.

Not long after the algebraic debacle, almost as compensation it seemed, Blair and Wint were sent on another special training course. This time they arrived at their destination to find that the course covered advanced flying for experienced pilots. The two men, of course, were yet to set foot inside an aircraft. 'Sometimes,' said John Blair later, 'it felt as if confusion reigned.'

Once again the pair was sent packing when this new mistake was recognized, but these shared experiences only served to reinforce their friendship.

Completing their period at McGill, the Jamaican pair of John Blair and Arthur Wint were now posted to what was known as the Initial Training Wing. This was more advanced than anything they had done before and the Wing had a very modern feel to it. The men knew that when they finished this stage of their training each would be assigned an area of specialization, becoming trainee pilots, navigators or bomb aimers. At this point John Blair's flying career almost ended before it got off the ground. Not long after he arrived, the men were told that they had to attend a flying medical. This medical was more difficult to pass than the basic medical all servicemen and women had to take. The friends had been out drinking in Montreal until four o'clock in the morning and almost as soon as they had arrived back at the Wing, John heard a voice call out, 'Blair! Medical!' Ten minutes later he had been washed out of aircrew as unfit.

John Blair was now an outcast. He was banished to what was known as the Holding School in Toronto, which was situated in an old exhibition hall made up of several huge buildings with bunk beds stretching away as far as the eye could see in every direction. John was depressed and lonely, perched on the edge of a cold, hard mattress, his head in his hands and his mind on what fate might now await him.

Within the Holding School there was a special office for RAF servicemen who had failed their courses and who were going to be sent back to England without any further flight training, but there was no equivalent arrangement for sending people back to the West Indies. It appeared that John Blair too would go to England without further training and in the company of all these strange Englishmen. He had never seen so many of them in one place. There were about five hundred men in John's hall alone and the whole facility held several thousand personnel waiting to be shipped home. John did not know a single soul in this huge assembly and he felt more alone and isolated than ever before.

After about three weeks cooling his heels and still feeling in low spirits, John went to see the Canadian Medical Officer. He told the medic his tale and the officer said, 'Alright, we'll give you another try.' He then ran a series of tests on John, most of which involved looking at various coloured pictures and reporting what he saw. The very next day John was given the full Air Force medical and two days later the matter was cleared up and he was on his way back to the training school, mightily relieved and smiling broadly.

John's grin faded when he realized that, having missed almost a month of classes, he would now be placed in a new group and that to make matters worse he was now the only West Indian on the course, all of his friends having gone on ahead. This was a new experience for John, but as it turned out it was not a problem at all and he felt that he was treated just like any other member of the class.

John Blair focused on the task at hand and eventually it was confirmed that he had indeed been selected for navigator training. This was quite a responsibility, because after the pilot, the navigator is the key man in any bomber crew and the brains of the aircraft. It is his job to get the crew to and from the target without leaving the safety of the bomber stream, for a lone bomber, lost over Europe, had a greatly reduced chance of survival. John would have to navigate the route at night using complicated scientific aids and he would often need to perform mathematical calculations while under enemy fire, bouncing around in a heavy bomber at 20,000 feet. But he felt he was up to the task.

At flight school John and his fellow students flew sixty-four hours by day and forty hours by night between 5 September 1942 and 28 January 1943, before they took their examinations and attempted to qualify. John passed the navigator's course, which included navigation, signals, aircraft recognition, photography, armament training, and day and night flying. It was an intensive, comprehensive programme, and the students worked seven days a week, but most found the training enjoyable. They were now increasingly confident about their potential. Even at this late stage, however, they were far from being ready for operations, no matter how cocky they might be feeling. In operational terms, these men were 'just toddlers learning to walk, less than half ready for the real thing'.

They trained on Anson aircraft, aged twin-engine planes with very limited navigational equipment. The equipment took the form of a map, a compass and a radio they had to tune in order to get a bearing. The Anson only had room for the pilot, the trainee navigator sitting behind him and a second trainee navigator who sat in the co-pilot's seat. Each navigator would work alone, alternating with the other trainee. Whoever was navigating would scribble directions on the course and airspeed for the pilot onto message pads and pass them to him. The second navigator would practice his map-reading and also wind the landing gear up after take-off and down before landing.

The crew squeezed into the aircraft, weighed down with all their gear, and then they sat there a while waiting for things to start. John was looking out of one of the windows at the little strip of runway beside them and thinking, 'What the hell am I doing here?' It was a question he was to ask himself many times over the next few years. The pilot went through his pre-flight procedures, flicking switches left, right and centre. Then the port engine made a kind of whining sound, followed by a splutter, with puffs of smoke being whirled around by the propellers. Finally, the engine roared into life and the whole aircraft started to vibrate. The pilot then went through the same procedure for the starboard engine, and before long the aircraft was rolling down the runway. They sped up painfully slowly, bumping along with the end of the runway clearly in view until, finally, the pilot heaved back on the stick and the aircraft clawed its way into the air. Still looking out of the window, John could see the buildings, roads and fields diminishing in size below him until they looked like little toy structures. This was his first time in the air!

The trainee crews did not go far on these early flights, each of which was a set piece event lasting between two and three hours as they navigated in a circle from waypoint to waypoint. The navigator had to know the aircraft's position at any time, regardless of bad weather or enemy action, so as to ensure the survival of aircraft and crew and this involved working constantly during a flight to keep the aircraft exactly on track and on schedule. A great deal of concentration was needed and with his head down over his maps and instruments for most of the flight, the only dialogue the navigator had with the rest of the crew would be to issue course instructions and exchange the odd terse remark.

Some men would die on their training flights, for flying in this era was a dangerous business, even without the presence of an enemy. Flight Sergeant Raymond Britto from Trinidad was killed on 2 January 1943 while flying with the 52 Operational Training Unit, Aston Down, in Spitfire AR240. He was 25-years-old. The short report on the incident simply says, 'Stalled on approach and crash-landed, Aston Down'. When his engine stalled, Raymond Britto attempted to glide the aircraft in, but it spun in instead, hitting the ground near the watchtower building. He is buried in Cirencester cemetery. Britto, who was presumably married and who had a daughter, flew for Fighter Command, but RAF Bomber Command would itself lose more than 8,000 men in training accidents like this one during the war.

During his own bomb aiming training and on his first flight with live ordinance, John Ebanks believed he had dropped his bomb on the target and the crew headed for home. As they were returning to base they realized that the aircraft was not handling properly; the bomb was still attached. Ebanks said to the pilot, 'I don't believe the bomb is gone!' At this stage they were flying at 20,000 feet and John suggested that they descend 10,000 feet because he suspected that ice might be the cause of the problem. When they had descended to 10,000 feet and returned to the target area he pressed the bomb release button again and the aircraft jumped up by over 1,000 feet as the bomb left the plane. After that experience Ebanks never had any doubts as to whether or not his bombs had been dropped.

Cy Grant's crew would later have a close escape on the morning of 5 May 1943, when their bomber aircraft suffered an engine failure on the return leg of a flight to Nantes, where they had dropped leaflets on the city. They crash-landed on Greenham Common, the nose of the aircraft ending up against the trunk of a large tree. The crew crawled out unscathed.

Once John Blair and his new group of friends had successfully completed the navigation phase of their training they were posted back to Moncton. On the way, Blair stopped off in Toronto and was amazed to see Arthur Wint at the railway station. Wint had appeared out of nowhere, big and tall, walking up to him. Both men were surprised, but happy to see each other. Like Blair, Wint was now wearing a little white flash on his cap, showing that he was a Flying Trainee and after a long period without the company of his countrymen, Blair was able to travel back to Moncton with Wint. Arthur Wint was now a pilot and John Blair was a navigator. It felt very good to know that they were part of a small group that had already achieved something really special, becoming commissioned as RAF officers and taking their place amongst the world's earliest black fliers. They stood tall and proud on the station platform.

When the pair arrived once more in Moncton it was bitterly cold and snowing heavily. Again they struggled through the snow with their gear to their old barrack room, where a sergeant reminded them that as they we were now officers they were entitled to live in the Officers' Mess. This was some distance away through the snow on the far side of the compound, but here they found themselves well taken care of and in pleasant company and they met up with several more Jamaicans who had also qualified, some for bomber squadrons and several as RAF fighter pilots.

Black Fighter Boys

The Caribbean volunteers joining Bomber Command were not the only, or even the first, black Caribbean flyers to go to war in Europe's skies. As we have seen, some of their compatriots were already serving as fighter pilots and more would follow. Fighter Command was the other half of the RAF. While the Bomber Command 'heavies' flew mostly at night, without fighter escort, to drop their bomb loads on the cities and factories of the German Reich, the men of Fighter Command fought primarily by day, although a smaller number of RAF night fighters also played an important role as interceptors, searching for German bombers and playing a deadly cat and mouse game with the German Nachtjager (night fighters).

Following the Allied victory in the Battle of Britain, fought in the air above the British Isles throughout the summer of 1940, Fighter Command had continued to go from strength to strength. RAF Spitfires, Hurricanes, Mosquitoes, Typhoons and other makes and models engaged the Luftwaffe units based in France through an ongoing series of fighter 'sweeps'. These large sorties by groups of aircraft were designed to draw the German fighters into the air to protect their bases in order that they might be engaged and shot down. Heavy raids on the Luftwaffe's airfields were also carried out repeatedly. This was a war of attrition and the Allies were winning, in large part because they could out produce their enemy.

The main role of a Second World War fighter aircraft was to shoot down other aircraft, and, when so tasked, to attack targets on the ground with rockets, cannon fire or small bombs. The main focus of an RAF fighter pilot during the middle part of the Second World War was therefore enemy fighters. This meant duelling one-on-one with the cream of the Luftwaffe, many of them experienced veterans with several years of flying and numerous victories to their credit.

Many Caribbean volunteer pilots took part in the Fighter Command campaign and Vincent Bunting was typical. Born in Panama in 1918, but raised in Kingston, Jamaica, when war broke out he was one of the early volunteers and after successfully completing his training he became a fighter pilot. Bunting initially joined No. 611 Squadron in December 1942, but after being promoted to the rank of warrant officer, he was transferred to No. 132 Squadron, which flew Spitfires from southern England. The squadron spent most of 1943 flying fighter sweeps over occupied France. After a short period providing defensive cover over Scotland in early 1944, No. 132 Squadron moved south again to join the 2nd Tactical Air Force, where it would conduct fighter-bomber operations against targets in northern France as part of the lead up to the D-Day landings in Normandy.

Bunting's squadron provided cover for the landing beaches themselves from 6 June 1944 and at the end of the month they moved their base to Normandy, within earshot of the fighting. This allowed them to spend more of their flight time over their targets, most of which were German army units, the Luftwaffe having now pulled back to defend Germany itself.

In October 1944, Bunting was transferred to No. 154 Squadron where he flew American built P51 Mustang fighters. On 27 March 1945, while leaded a section from his squadron, Bunting destroyed an enemy aircraft near Lubeck in Germany. In 1945 he was commissioned as a pilot officer, and in June of that year he received his last flying post in the RAF when he joined No. 1 Squadron, one of the first four squadrons formed at the birth of the Royal Flying Corps in 1912. By the end of the Second World War, Bunting was engaged in flying long-range escort missions over Germany, protecting the heavy bombers on their way to and from their targets.

Flight Sergeant James Hyde, of San Juan, Trinidad, also arrived in Britain in 1942 and he too became a Spitfire pilot. Hyde flew operationally in 1944 with No. 132 Squadron during the Normandy campaign, flying alongside Vincent Bunting, but his days were numbered. At 1525 hours on 25 September 1944, Hyde took off in his Spitfire to provide air cover during the battle of Arnhem, the Allied attempt to secure bridges over the Rhine River as a gateway into Germany itself. Hyde's flight was attacked by enemy aircraft from Luftwaffe Jagdkorps II (Fighter Corps Two) and he was shot down and killed during a dogfight over Nijmegen, one of four Spitfire pilots claimed on the same day near that city. Hyde is buried in Jonkerbos War Cemetery, Holland. He was 27-years-old when he died.

Pilot Officer Collins Joseph also volunteered in 1941 and qualified as a Spitfire pilot, serving with No. 130 Squadron. The son of Elmie Joseph, of San Fernando, Trinidad, Joseph went missing at 1530 hours on 31 December 1944, while on an air operation flying the route Liege, Aachen, Liege. There is no corresponding German claim for a Spitfire in that area on that date, so it is possible that Joseph fell victim either to flak or mechanical failure. He was 28-years-old and is buried at the Hotton War Cemetery in Belgium.

Victor Emmanuel Tucker was a bright Jamaican graduate of a Methodist boarding school in Kingston. In 1934, at the age of seventeen, he travelled to England to study at the Bar. The son of Adrian and Lydia Tucker, he later qualified as a Barrister-at-Law and married Wilhelmina Casimir Chrenko Tucker, who is thought to have been from Highgate, in the Jamaican Parish of St Mary. Already in Great Britain when war broke out, Tucker volunteered early for the RAF and was accepted for pilot training. By 1942 he was a flight sergeant with No. 129 Squadron. On 21 October 1941, Tucker was wounded in action and his Spitfire was heavily damaged during a fighter sweep over France.

Tucker returned to service and on 4 May 1942, his squadron was escorting RAF Boston medium bombers on a raid to Le Harve when they were attacked from above by Luftwaffe Focke-Wulf 190 fighter aircraft, at the time the most advanced German fighter in service. Tucker's squadron leader ordered his fighters to abort the escort mission and fly a left turn. The pilots protested, as this manoeuvre would give the German fighters the advantage of attacking them out of the sun, blinding the RAF pilots. Nevertheless, the order stood. The squadron turned left and the German pilots duly dived out of the sun, fired their cannon and Flight Sergeant Tucker was shot down and killed, his aircraft crashing in the English Channel off Octeville-sur-Mer. His was one of sixteen Spitfires shot down by the Luftwaffe on the same date. Victor Tucker was 25-years-old.

These pioneers were probably unaware of the fact that others had in fact gone before them. From the United States the eccentric character of Eugene Bullard had flown with the French Air Force over the western front during the First World War, and, even earlier in 1915, Ahmet Ali Çelikten had flown with the forces of the Ottoman Empire. Çelikten, was a half Nigerian, half Turk pilot who did part of his flying training in Berlin and was almost certainly the world's first black pilot. A black Jamaican flyer named William Robinson Clarke also flew as an RE-8 pilot with the British Royal Flying Corps over the Western Front in 1917, becoming the first black West Indian to fly in combat.

Eugene Bullard, from Georgia, was the son of William O. Bullard (nicknamed 'Big Chief Ox') and Josephine Thomas, a Creek Indian. Bullard, the last of ten children, left the US and initially made his home in Aberdeen, Scotland, where he became a boxer and a music hall performer. He later moved to Paris and at the start of the First World War he joined the French Foreign Legion. Wounded at the bloody and horrific battle of Verdun in 1916, and a recipient of the Croix de Guerre, he then joined the Lafayette Flying Corps in 1917 and flew twenty combat missions, claiming two kills and gaining the sobriquet 'The Black Swallow of Death'. As soon as America entered the war, Bullard volunteered for service in the US Army Air Service, but he was rejected on the basis of his race.

When Germany again invaded France in 1940, Bullard joined French troops in the defence of Orléans and was wounded in the spine. Bullard survived and returned to the United States with his two daughters (he had married, then divorced, but gained custody of the girls). He died in obscurity in 1961, a stranger in his own country, having been badly beaten and permanently injured in a racial attack after a concert in New York in 1949.

Ignored in his homeland, Bullard was better remembered in France and in 1954 the French government invited him to help rekindle the everlasting flame at the Tomb of the Unknown Soldier under the Arc de Triomphe in Paris. Then in 1959 he was made a Chevalier of the Légion d'honneur, that nation's highest decoration.

At the time of the First World War, the recruitment of black military personnel for fighting roles in the British armed forces was highly controversial, despite the long standing existence of black regiments in the West Indies and Africa, and of a large number of Indian regiments, several of the latter serving for a period in the trenches on the Western Front. *The People* – a British newspaper – asked as late as 14 January 1917, *'should our dusky warriors play a bigger part in smashing the huns?'* and stated: *'we are told that the way to win the war is to turn loose millions of black men,* [but] *... it is dangerous to teach the black ... when we have expended money and time upon the making of an army, that army would be very likely to turn upon its creators'*.

Nevertheless, at least one black West Indian was determined to overcome these objections and fly in battle. William Robinson ('Robbie') Clarke was born in Kingston, Jamaica in 1895 and he grew up on the south coast of the island, later working as a chauffeur at a time when very few people owned cars. He almost certainly worked for an important colonial officer, plantation owner or businessman and we can speculate that this might have been a factor in his successful efforts to join the Royal Flying Corps in July 1915.

Clarke traveled to England without official assistance and volunteered his services on arrival. He was accepted and for the first year of his service Clarke was engaged as an aircraft mechanic, maintaining the aircraft that flew against the Germans. It is likely that his skills as a driver, still a rare thing in 1915, were a key factor in his color being overlooked by the recruiters. Posted to France as a driver and mechanic, Clarke now had close contact with the men who flew the planes, and with the aircraft themselves. Some historians have speculated that he may even have been allowed to experience flying as a passenger, perhaps by a sympathetic officer.

Whatever the reasons, Clarke was accepted onto a course for aviation instruction in 1916, finally realizing his dream of flight. His training was conducted back in England and by May 1917 he was posted to Belgium to join 4th Squadron Royal Flying Corps as a fully qualified pilot with the rank of sergeant. The squadron was based at Abeele, not far behind the British front lines at Ypres, where fighting had been going on since 1914. This area of the front had been devastated by continual shelling over three years and it comprised a complex spidersweb offering all of the horrors and the Dantesque scenery that has come to represent the First World War. It was over this panorama of torn and bruised earth that Robbie Clarke would now fly a Reconnaisance Experimental 8, or RE-8, a two-seater biplane and the most widely used aircraft of its type during the war.

One of the war's most famous battles was about the commence, the Battle of Messines Ridge. The German army had been entrenched on this rising ground for three full years and was deeply dug in, overlooking the Allied lines. The Allies had devised a ruthless plan for removing the enemy and seizing this dominating ground for themselves. Units of miners, specially recruited from the coalfields of the Empire, had dug entensive shafts and tunnels deep into the heart of the hills on which the Germans sat. They had then packed the tunnels with hundreds of tons of explosives at key points all along the German line. At a prearranged time, the mines were all detonated simultaneously, tearing huge craters in the ridgeline, vaporizing many of the defenders and sending the dismembered bodies of hundreds of others tumbling high into the air, along with countless tons of soil and rock. At that moment, the British infantry left their trenches, crossed no-man's-land and seized the ridge, gathering up the dazed and shell-shocked German survivors of the massive blasts.

The Royal Flying Corps played a vital role in this operation by flying directly over the German trenches to take detailed aerial photographs of the defences that could be used by the men planning the attack. These reconnaisance flights exposed the flyers to danger from enemy ground fire, as well as to attack by defending German aircraft. They were also under threat from their own side, for the British aircraft were forced to fly under the trajectory of the Allied artillery barrage, with heavy shells flying through the air around them. Clarke reported that one shell passed so close to the aircraft he was piloting that it clipped one of the wires that ran between the upper and lower wing. Had it hit the engine of the plane they would have simply evaporated like many of the Germans on the ridge below were destined to do.

With Messines Ridge now firmly in British hands, Clarke continued his reconnaisance flights along the new front line. His luck ran out in July 1917, when five German aircraft attacked from above while Clarke and his Observer were searching for a target to bomb, having already taken photographs of German positions five miles behind the front line. Their aircraft was riddled with bullets. Although the Observer was unhurt, one

German bullet passed through Clarke's spine and came out under his arm. He was also hit in several places on his back and in the face by splinters from his own aircraft, but he was able to pilot his aircraft almost back to base. He was too weak to continue and eventually landed in a field, from which he was rescued and taken to hospital. Having saved both his own life and that of his Observer, Clarke was not released from hospital until November that year and his four month stay provides an indication of how serious his injuries must have been.

Although Clarke never returned to flying, having been too badly hurt and medically downgraded, he remained with the RFC for the duration of the war, resuming his role as an air mechanic. In 1919, he was repatriated to Kingston, Jamaica, at the expense of the British government, who also refunded him the cost of his original voluntary journey to Britain. With a substantial one-off award of £60, in lieu of a pension, Clarke sank back into obscurity, living until he was reportedly in his eighties. Clarke's name is virtually unknown – even in Jamaica – yet he was one of the most important pioneers of black aviation and integration within what would later become the Royal Air Force.

Chapter 4

The Mediterranean Theatre; I Will Have None of that Nonsense; Part of Something Big

Although the voyage of the Trinidadian passengers on the *Strathallan* had been uneventful, the ship and her crew would not be so fortunate. In late 1942 the *Strathallan* took part in Operation Torch, the Allied landings in North Africa that eventually led to the ejection of the Axis forces from the continent. SS *Strathallan* left the Clyde on what would be her last trip on 11 December 1942, carrying more than 4,000 troops, 250 nurses, 430 crewmen and General Eisenhower's Headquarters.

At about 0230 hours on 21 December 1942, U-boat Kapitänleutnant Horst Hamm raised the periscope of his submarine, U562, and spotted the outline of a large passenger liner. Patrolling the North African coast near Oran, U562 and its crew of forty-nine officers and men were on their seventh war patrol. It was Hamm's second U-boat command and in November 1941 he had taken the vessel through the dangerous Straits of Gibraltar, which were heavily patrolled by the British Royal Navy, after just one patrol in the Atlantic. The boat, which was now based at La Spezia, fired a single torpedo at the target.

According to Hamm's log, two hits were heard and it was believed that the *Strathalan* may also have been under attack from German or Italian aircraft and that it suffered its second hit from an airborne torpedo. The ship was badly damaged and two engineering officers and two engine room crewmen were killed. A conflicting report puts the total number killed at six. After being taken in tow by another vessel, the *Strathallan* caught fire and she turned over and sank twelve miles from Oran the following day. Survivors recalled the actions of one RAF Flight Lieutenant Dodd. This very brave officer was one of several heroic passengers on the *Strathallan*, who, without regard for their own safety, dived into the oily water surrounding the stricken ship rescuing others in distress.

Hamm and his crew returned safely to their base, despite being depth charged by the Luftwaffe on route in a 'friendly fire' incident, there being nothing friendly about fire of this type. In February 1943, Hamm and his crew ventured further east across the Mediterranean to attack shipping near the British port of Alexandria in Egypt, but the submarine was spotted from the air by an RAF Wellington bomber. The bomber and two British destroyers launched a series of depth charge attacks on U562 and she was sunk on the 19 February. There were no survivors.

The success of Operation Torch, combined with the victory of British and Commonwealth troops over Rommel's Africa Korps at the battle of El Alamein, had driven the Axis forces in North Africa into a stoutly defended pocket in Tunisia. After a bitter struggle, the remaining force, over a quarter of a million strong, finally surrendered and Allied aircraft were now able to prepare the way for an invasion of Sicily and then Italy, thus opening a second front in Europe. The winter of 1942–43 had also seen the encirclement and eventual surrender of another huge Axis force at Stalingrad, deep inside Soviet Russia, and these two developments represented a turning point in the conflict that was apparent to most thinking people at the time. From now on, the Allies would be on the offensive for most of the remainder of the war.

The bombing operations conducted from North Africa against targets in the Mediterranean and south-east Europe were very different from those conducted against northern France, the Low Countries and Germany itself. Most Mediterranean operations were carried out by lighter twin engine bombers such as the Wellington and the targets were smaller and better defined. There was very little cause to carpet bomb cities, and raids against factories, ports, enemy airfields, rail junctions and troop concentrations were the main focus. This in turn meant that the bombers had to fly at lower altitudes, typically bombing from 10,000 feet or lower, and that made the entire proposition just as hazardous to life and limb as operations over northern Europe. Raids penetrated as far as the strategically vital Romanian oilfields at Ploesti and often met fierce resistance.

Night operations were often illuminated by flares, which would light up the target, but also reveal the attacking aircraft. Some pilots employed the practice of dropping each bomb individually, flying over a target ten or fifteen times until the last bomb had gone and then returning so that the gunners could attack with machine-gun fire. This was no Mediterranean cruise and losses in the air were high.

David Chance of Jamaica had attended the well regarded Munro College on that island before joining the RAF in 1941 while in the United Kingdom. After training in Canada, he returned to England as a pilot officer in 1943, before being posted to Gambut in Libya as a Beaufighter pilot with 603 Squadron. Flying from Libya, Chance engaged in strike operations against German and Italian shipping in the Mediterannean and Aegean before being transferred, in January 1945, to pilot the Mosquito fighter-bomber with 248 Squadron, on anti-shipping raids off the coasts of Denmark and Norway. These raids were swift and deadly. Coming in low and at high speed, the Mosquitos would fire their rockets and heavy machine guns at the enemy ships, sending plumes of water, bright orange and red fireballs and mushrooms of dark smoke, high into the air from the exploding vessels. Sometimes the aircraft were so low that they flew through the smoke of the burning hulks as they passed overhead. RAF attacks of this nature were so effective that German naval operations in both theatres virtually ceased.

Osmund Alleyne of Dominica also joined the RAF in 1941 and trained as a wireless operator and air gunner. By mid-1943 he was a flight sergeant serving with 142 'Cuty' Squadron, so named after its 'QT' lettering, which operated Wellingtons. Based in North Africa, Alleyne was serving aboard Wellington X HE629 and flying missions over Sicily and southern Italy.

Conditions on the North African airbases were primitive and the men lived in tents, enduring daytime temperatures of over one hundred degrees, which could drop below freezing at night, and risking bites or stings from snakes and scorpions, while swatting away clouds of flies. During the frequent dust storms visibility would drop to zero and dust would get everywhere, clogging the nose, eyes and mouth, damaging aircraft engines and generally making life hell for all concerned. Any rain would then turn the landing fields and tented areas into a miserable quagmire and since all aircraft maintenance had to be performed in the open air, the ground crews suffered as much from the weather, if not more, than the aircrew.

Food was often supplemented with local meat and other produce and many of the men experienced severe stomach complaints. Essentials were in short supply; beds, tents, latrine materials and all manner of utensils had to be scrounged or stolen. Malaria, dysentery, jaundice and a range of similar ailments had men queuing at the medical tent each day.

The airstrips themselves were normally situated on barren plains, far removed from any form of civilization. There was nothing exotic about such a posting and even the most adventurous of men found that life in this particular foreign clime quickly lost its charm. All they wanted was to get the war over with as quickly as possible so that they could all go home. Talk centred on the joys of London, or Sydney, or Toronto, the taste of a decent beer (warm or cold, depending on the man's origins) and the embrace of a decent (or not so decent) woman.

The Wellington bomber had only meagre defences and unescorted it was easy prey for enemy fighters. In his book *Bloody Biscay*, author Chris Goss quotes an account by Luftwaffe pilot Uffz-Unteroffizier Heinz Hommel of an engagement with one of three such Wellington bombers, two of which were shot down:

'On 1 June 1943, I was flying as wingman to Oberstleutnant Horstmann. After sighting the Wellington, my leader climbed over the enemy plane and attacked from the front and above. I had to break off my first attack because of the enemy plane's evasive actions and I had got into its rear turret's field of fire and got a lot of machine-gun fire. During this first action, my plane was hit by one bullet in the port wing. A short time after that, I was able to get into a favourable position and attacked head on from above, watching the cannon and machine gun hits in the enemy plane's starboard wing. From a distance of 100 meters, I saw a tongue of fire coming out from the starboard wing which became even larger. Soon the whole wing was ablaze and then broke off. The plane went into a spin and exploded on hitting the water. I saw the rear gunner bailing out, but his parachute was also burning. No survivors were seen, only wreckage.'

On the night of 5/6 August 1943, Flight Sergeant Alleyne's squadron formed part of a force assigned to bomb Cap Peloro in the north-east corner of Sicily, on the Messina Straits. The squadron was to bomb the beach areas because large numbers of enemy troops had been spotted in barges attempting to cross from Sicily to the Italian mainland. The aircraft took off without incident at 2350 hours and arrived over the target area at 0220 hours, bombing from a height of between 5,000 and 8,000 feet. Although the target was illuminated with flares, cloud obstructed the attackers' view and the effects of the bombs dropped could not be easily discerned. The defences were described as 'light', but four RAF bombers failed to return that night, including that of Flight Sergeant Alleyne, who is remembered on the Malta Memorial. A monument to the 2,298 Commonwealth aircrew who lost their lives in the Second World War air battles around the Mediterranean and who have no known grave, can be found in the area named Floriana, to the south side of the Triton Fountain and close to City Gate, the entrance to Malta's capital, Valletta.

Alleyne's entire crew died with him, five men in total. Alleyne was not the only Caribbean volunteer to serve in this theatre and he appears to have spent at least some of his service in the company of one J. Rowan Henry of Antigua.

The Caribbean volunteers were joined in the region by the now famous US 99th Fighter Squadron (originally Pursuit Squadron), first of the 'Tuskegee Airmen', and a short time later by the US 332 Fighter Group, which contained a further three black fighter squadrons. These segregated black American fighter units were the first of that nation to serve in any conflict and they flew with distinction until the end of the war. Unlike the RAF fliers, however, they were never allowed to serve alongside whites and they experienced discrimination from many of their own countrymen throughout the war. By way of example, black crews at one training base in the USA in Seymour, Indiana, found that while the local laundries were willing to wash the clothes of German prisoners of war, they refused to accept those belonging to serving black US Army Air Force pilots, all of whom were American citizens.

I will have none of that nonsense
Although John Blair and Arthur Wint were now RAF officers, they were still very junior, and, like the remainder of the population, they only heard

about the war's progress through the newspapers and radio reports. It was now January 1944 and while they knew that the Allies were winning the war, it was evident that there was still a long, hard struggle ahead and a high price yet to pay. With all the training they had been through they were now just hoping to get into front line action before the war ended.

At last the two friends were ordered to board ship once more, this time bound for Britain and action. Arthur Wint and John Blair travelled together, but most of the other Caribbean volunteers had by now long disappeared, sent off to their various units. Several were already dead. They sailed from Halifax in Canada, to Glasgow in Scotland, on a huge troopship packed to the brim with soldiers and airmen. On this voyage they were not stuck in the hold, but space below decks was very limited all the same. During the voyage the men did not see another vessel, for in order to avoid the U-boat threat, the ship sailed a course far to the north, skirting Iceland before turning south again towards the British Isles.

On arrival in Glasgow, Blair and Wint were given forms to take to the local tailor. They were measured for their new officer's uniforms, which were a great improvement on the uncomfortable kit they had been wearing up to that point. The men were due for some leave, but before they could head out into public view they wanted to get themselves properly dressed.

Now that they were wearing RAF uniforms with aircrew insignia, these two black volunteers experienced very few negative reactions from the people they met at their British RAF base. On the contrary, people seemed both surprised and pleased to see them. It was, however, a very strange feeling for the pair when they first put on their new uniforms and walked into an English pub full of white patrons. A few pints quickly gave them some relief and they found that people expressed gratitude for their sacrifice. It soon became normal for them to walk into any pub full of strangers and within a few moments have someone walk over and say 'Please have a beer with me'. This was Yorkshire and John Blair would always have fond memories of these 'kind and friendly people'.

Jamaican Billy Strachan described the response he received in British civilian circles:

'When you arrived anywhere as (the first) black man you were treated like a teddy bear. You were loved and fêted.'

Harry McCalla, a self-described 'coloured' man from Jamaica said, 'It was all right until the English became aware of colour. About 1955 or 56, I'd say. I had difficulty getting a flat then. There were so many immigrants coming in.'

The men had overcome the initial hurdles of ingrained racism and ignorance and had now established themselves as deserving of respect and even admiration for their bravery in volunteering and providing a service that was not required of them. In several cases, arrangements were even made for the men to spend weekends in the homes of British families as part of their orientation, and when in London they had access to special RAF accommodation and leisure facilities.

Other black volunteers spoke of how English girls would come out of their homes to watch as the athletes among the men passed on their training runs. At the dances that were held regularly, a fit, good looking man from the Caribbean would often find himself dancing with the prettiest girl present. Several of the airmen eventually married their English girlfriends, and some took them home to the islands, while others chose to raise their families in Britain.

It wasn't all smooth sailing. When John Ebanks first entered the Sergeant's Mess at his new base, a cluster of English servicemen standing by the bar muttered complaints and, turning their backs on him, began to move away. At that moment, a senior Non-Commissioned Officer (NCO) gruffly ordered, 'Get back here you lot. I will have none of that nonsense in my Mess.' John reported that he never experienced any further overt hostility during his time with the RAF, but it was clear that there were still many unresolved issues simmering below the surface and these would re-emerge at the highest levels of the RAF's hierarchy towards the end of the war.

Cy Grant found that the British people were generally friendly, although children would occasionally point him out to their mothers in the street. But the prevailing attitude seems to have been one of curiosity rather than hostility. As he put it, there was a war on and he was in RAF uniform. He was on their side. Grant reported that he never experienced any overt racism in the RAF itself. Eyebrows were raised the first time he entered his own Officers' Mess, but he was quickly accepted once it was established that he could, in fact, speak English clearly.

Asked how he dealt with racial remarks and prejudice during the war, Jamaican Billy Strachan replied:

'It was there, all right. But my own experience, together with that of most of my colleagues, showed that whenever one black person arrived anywhere, he was always welcomed and treated well. Two, they coped with. It was when three or more arrived that racism really got sharp. I know that some of us fared badly, but I had no problems in that respect.'

As we shall see, a few black airmen were about to experience and endure what is perhaps the most racist environment that has ever existed. Their ability to survive in such circumstances was soon to be tested to extremes.

As far as the RAF itself was concerned, the recruitment of Caribbean aircrew had been a success story. Hundreds of well educated, fit young men had joined up to fight and both in training and on operations they were fitting in and performing as well as their white colleagues. The following excerpt from a progress report produced on 18 May 1945 summarizes how the aircrew volunteers were officially perceived:

Confidential
Coloured RAF personnel: report on progress and suitability

… West Indians, were enlisted at Moncton between the end of 1942 and May 1944 when overseas aircrew recruiting was suspended, and a close examination has been made of the aircrew training, and other reports of eighty of this number.

    (a)   There were no suspensions and the ground and air percentages of 'Above Average' and 'Below Average' suggest that they fall very much in line with the white trainee.

(b) There were very few instances of the standard of discipline being criticized.

(c) Description of temperament was so varied that it is impossible to classify the contingent as a whole. The term 'quiet' and even 'docile' is used frequently, but it must be borne in mind that these reports deal with a comparatively early stage when they may not have had time to find their feet.

(d) Sixteen of the cases under review were assessed as 'Below Average' in Character and Leadership, and eighteen (seven of whom were recommended for commissions) as 'Above Average'. The remarks in the previous sub-paragraph may have some bearing on the large number classified under the lower assessment...

...

(i) The West Indian personnel selected for training have proved themselves capable of reaching and maintaining the high technical standard required from operational aircrew and that their discipline, team spirit and general conduct is such as to enable them to carry out the ground duties required of an officer or NCO with complete satisfaction.

Part of the fitting in to life in the RAF that needed to take place required the West Indians to learn the special language of the Air Force. Many people, particularly the more senior officers, really did talk in a fashion that nowadays one only hears in old black and white films. This manner of speech became a habit for men like John Blair and later, when he returned home, it caused some amusement. Words like 'chaps', 'prang' and 'old kite' simply had no equivalent in Caribbean culture and they seemed particularly out of place when coming from a black man's mouth.

It took the volunteers a fortnight to get fully kitted out, but as soon as they had achieved this they all headed into London to enjoy three week's well deserved leave. The RAF had reserved hotels for its personnel in the city, and they were given free accommodation in one of these. They spent their time touring the war damaged city and seeing its famous sights for the first time, reinforced and refreshed by the occasional drink.

At the end of their leave, Arthur Wint and John Blair returned to their base in Yorkshire and then were sent on a Battle Course at RAF Filey. This course included the use of weapons in combat and many other aspects of infantry combat training. The course of instruction was intended to prepare them for the possibility of being shot down over enemy territory and having to fight to survive, although in practice few RAF aircrew would opt to fight on landing after escaping from their burning aircraft. On completing this course, they were back onto Anson aircraft for familiarization flying over the UK at RAF Wigtown in Scotland. There was indeed a big difference between navigating the wide open spaces of Canada, where it had been relatively difficult to lose their way, and flying over England where there was a new town every few miles and where the blackout was in operation at night. They found this new territory much more confusing and challenging and the familiarization flying course was essential to their survival.

The trainees were closer than ever to the day when they would have to go to war and once the familiarization training was finished John Blair was posted to an Operational Training Unit at RAF Kinloss, located near the village of the same name, on the Moray Firth in the north of Scotland. This was the place at which pilots, engineers, gunners, and bomb aimers would team up to form the crews who would then fly and fight together for the duration of their first 'tour' of thirty missions.

A large group of men, pilots, navigators, flight engineers, wireless operators, bomb aimers and air gunners, assembled in a huge, cold and echoing aircraft hangar. Nobody present knew more than a few of the other people in the group. The pilots were then told to pick the rest of their crew and they all walked around choosing people they liked the look of.

Cy Grant went through the crewing up process at No. 30 OTU Hixon:

'Here I teamed up with my Captain, Flying Officer Alton Langille, a French Canadian who chose me to be his navigator, as he was to choose all the other crew members – because we were the best at our respective trades among the new batch of aircrew.'

The resulting crew of Lancaster W4827, Grant's aircraft, was typical of many Commonwealth crews at the time:

Pilot:	Flying Officer Al Langille (Canada)
Navigator:	Pilot Officer Cy Grant (British Guyana)
Wireless operator:	Pilot Officer Don Towers (England)
Bomb aimer:	Pilot Officer Charles Reynolds (England)
Flight engineer:	Sergeant Ronald Hollywood (England)
Air gunner:	Geoffrey Wallis (England)
Air gunner:	Pilot Officer Joseph Addison (Canada)

John Blair was also the only West Indian present during his 'crewing up' process, as none of the other Caribbean volunteers had been posted to Kinloss with him. He stood there in the noisy hangar and eventually a Canadian pilot, who was older than the average and very soft spoken, came up to him and asked, 'Will you come and fly with me?' This man was Ralph Pearson, who would be John's pilot and the leader of their crew from that point forward. Pearson, with John in tow, then selected two air gunners, one of whom was an Englishman named Morris, a wireless operator and a flight engineer named Laurie Wilder. The bomb aimer would join them later and he also turned out to be a Canadian.

They were all strangers in this crew of seven, but John felt that, although haphazard, it was an effective process. At the same time, the men were now going off to war with a group of strangers, without so much as a formal introduction. Of course, they would soon get to know each other very well indeed and the strangers would each become human, with good points and bad, and with their individual strengths and weaknesses.

To start the process of building crew cohesion, the men were now assigned to another old aircraft, a twin-engine Whitley. The Armstrong Whitley was one of three British front line medium bombers serving with the RAF at the outbreak of the war and its class had taken part in the first bombing attacks on German territory. Ordered in bulk as an urgent replacement for the biplane bombers still in RAF service as late as 1935, the Whitley continued to be part of the bombing campaign until it was itself replaced by larger four engine aircraft. Those four engine Lancaster and Halifax bombers would form the bulk of the Bomber Command operational force by 1944, with the older aircraft like the Whitley being used for training and other second line roles.

They spent four weeks flying that old Whitley, and when John Blair looked back on it years later he could only say that they must have been mad. It was an old aircraft, but luckily it was tough. Although the Whitley was solidly built, it was designed using pre-war technical knowledge and this was by now a very modern war. The Whitley and other aircraft of its generation, although less than ten years old, were outdated relics of a bygone era.

Fifty hours of flying is not much time to prepare to fight with a new crew and the men had to learn quickly. As the navigator, John was now using a radio system called Gee. This gave him directional readings from a beam transmitted from the ground, but they still had none of the new radar systems that some of the heavy bombers were equipped with. By using the Gee radio bearing, taking quick looks out of the window to plot their track on the ground (when cloud cover permitted) and by reading their weather reports in order to predict the flow of the wind, the navigators somehow guided their bomb-laden aircraft all the way to Germany and back with a fair degree of precision.

Part of something big

'The aim of the Combined Bomber Offensive should be unambiguously stated; the destruction of German cities, the killing of German workers, and the disruption of civilized life throughout Germany.'

Arthur Harris, Bomber Command

They knew they were involved in something big. The RAF Bomber Command airfields were part of an industrialized process, a vast conveyor belt with armaments factories at one end and German cities and industrial centres at the other. The point at which the bombs fell off the end of the belt and down through the freezing air onto their targets was occupied by the bomber force itself. Further back along the belt were the aircraft flying to the target through flak and fighter attacks and somewhere near the middle of the belt were the airfields from which they took off. The factories sat at the start of the belt and they fed bombs, bullets, aircraft and fuel into these bases, along with the training schools that fed in the men who would crew the planes or deliver the logistical support.

Because a thousand bombers flying alongside one another would represent a formation that was many miles wider than the largest German city, the aircraft flew to their targets as a stream, a few aircraft wide, but hundreds of aircraft long. The bomber stream was further broken down into waves. Each bomber was allotted a time slot and a height band and as a result not all aircraft would travel at precisely the same height. Missions were flown in the dark and despite the presence of hundreds of other planes in the air around them most crews could see little and it was possible to feel very alone and very exposed when flying over enemy territory. Any aircraft that accidentally left this three dimensional river of flying explosive force was likely to become easy prey for the enemy fighters prowling the night skies, like sharks looking for easy kills. The best Luftwaffe night fighter pilots could bring down four or five RAF bombers in a single night, sometimes more.

While the bomber stream protected the bombers from the enemy fighters, by both overwhelming them with concentrated numbers of planes and by creating opportunities for the RAF air gunners from two or more aircraft to focus their machine guns on one attacker, it also increased the risk of catastrophic airborne collisions. The timing, density and size of the bomber stream was carefully calculated to balance the estimated loss from fighter intercepts of bombers flying individually to the target, against the actual losses from collisions and flak in such a way that the latter figure was always the lower one.

This avenging industrialized behemoth was overseen from on high by Air Officer Commanding-in-Chief, Arthur Travers Harris, often known as 'Bomber Harris' by the press and public, but more commonly as 'Butcher Harris' by his RAF crews. His nickname reflected both his insistence on crews flying to dangerous targets in the face of heavy losses and his ruthless and unwavering commitment to the complete destruction of urban Germany. Harris was a man with a mission and that mission was to ensure that Germany would never again threaten the peace of Europe, both because its capacity to do so would have been eliminated, but also because the punishment meted out for its barbarous actions would deter any future aggression.

Harris explained his bombing strategy in the following terms:

'The aim of the Combined Bomber Offensive ... should be unambiguously stated [as] the destruction of German cities, the killing of German workers, and the disruption of civilized life throughout Germany ... the destruction of houses, public utilities, transport and lives, the creation of a refugee problem on an unprecedented scale, and the breakdown of morale both at home and at the battle fronts by fear of extended and intensified bombing, are accepted and intended aims of our bombing policy. They are not by-products of attempts to hit factories.'

This uncompromising statement of intent, though not made public at the time, clearly reflected the reality of the missions planned, executed and duly reported by Bomber Command during the second half of the war. Amongst the bomber crews, who could feel the heat of the firestorms raging in the centres of the cities they were attacking, and on some occasions even smell the smoke, few men can have doubted what the effects of their actions were. They had, after all, walked the streets of English cities subjected to raids that delivered German bombs onto those targets and the German V1 and V2 flying bombs and rockets continued to rain down by the thousand.

As a key link in the offensive chain, the typical RAF bomber base was the size of a small town. The new arrivals were initially bewildered by the complex of structures, some ultra modern but others surprisingly ramshackle, each with its own nomenclature and function. Only after several weeks would the logic of the arrangements start to become clear, as the men learned how each part of the whole acted to put them into the air, fuelled, fed and armed, and to propel them towards their targets.

Built on hard, well drained land somewhere in central or eastern England, from where targets in north–west and central Europe could be struck, each airfield was normally surrounded by a wire fence, often breached at numerous points where staff had created shortcuts. The main entrance was protected by sentry boxes with Military Police or other armed servicemen on duty. Just beyond the entrance sat the guard hut in which duty NCOs and off duty sentries would sit, snoozing, drinking tea and filling in their logs. The men of the guard knew a great deal about the base's occupants; who came and went, who returned drunk or sober, who came to visit and who tried to sneak back in late, perhaps with lipstick on his collar and a guilty smirk on his face. On the whole, aircrew were treated leniently; everyone knew that for many, perhaps for most, their remaining days were numbered.

The residents of the surrounding villages could see the vast, flat surfaces of the runways, beside which the cuboid shape of the control tower sat, painted military green and sprouting radio antennae. Beyond that stood sets of massive rectangular hangars, each large enough to house a four engine bomber for maintenance or repair. When not undergoing major work, the bombers stood on circular concrete pans around the airfield, looking like prehistoric beasts in their reptilian colours of black, brown and green.

By day, men swarmed around the aircraft, fixing, testing, cleaning, refuelling, checking and arming each one. The huge engines were started up and revved, their roars filling the air and would have been audible for miles around. Like a gathering of squat green pigs, dozens of corrugated-iron Nissen huts housed the aircrew, ground crew and a plethora of offices and administrative functions. Stores, medical services, planning, briefing and training rooms, the mysterious command blocks and the out of bounds married quarters were just some of the dozens of sign-posted, telephone-linked, buzzing hives of activity. The airfield was as busy as a football ground on the day of a cup final, except that this particular cup final took place on several nights of any given week.

During the daytime, bombers and crews would undertake regular test flights, describing broad circles over the surrounding countryside and monitoring the performance of the aircraft and its engines, before coming in to land on the long, wide runway of their home base. Once testing was complete it was time to arm the aircraft if operations were on for that night. Caravans of bombs snaked their way across the field from the bomb stores to the planes, bombs of all shapes and sizes, dark and lethal, pulled along by small tractors that were often driven by female ground crew.

Ulric Cross had completed his training and qualified as a Bomber Command navigator:

'From November 1941 to November 1942, I trained at Cranwell on the wireless, did meteorology, bomb aiming, navigation and Morse code. I graduated as a pilot officer and was assigned to Bomber Command.

I served as a navigator in the Pathfinder section of 139 Squadron; the famous 'Jamaica Squadron' of the RAF. The pathfinders led the way on bombing raids and marked the target; a most dangerous task. Our unit flew the famous Mosquito bomber, which was made mainly of wood. Jamaica had paid for many of the planes of 139 Squadron, hence the name. There was also a Trinidad Squadron, where Trinidad had paid for those planes. I was the only West Indian on my squadron. I was lucky to have served at fixed pre-war bases such as Marham, Wyton and Upwood. These fixed bases were more comfortable. There were many other temporary bases which had been scattered across the United Kingdom.

'My most harrowing mission was when one of the engines of our Mosquito fighter-bomber was shot up over Germany and we came down to 7,000 feet from 35,000 feet. We struggled back to England and crash landed in a quarry. It was a narrow escape but we made it out alive.'

John Ebanks flew from RAF Oakington, five miles north-west of Cambridge and well situated for visits to that city. Serving as a navigator with 571 Pathfinder Squadron, John also flew in Mosquito fighter-bombers. The task of the Pathfinders was to fly over the target ahead of the main bomber force and mark it with incendiaries and flares for the heavy bombers that followed them. No. 571 Squadron originally formed in April 1944 at Downham Market, as a light bomber unit of No. 8 (Pathfinder) Group. Equipped to carry bombs of sizes up to 4,000lbs, the squadron was designed and trained to conduct night raids with the Light Night Striking Force, most frequently being used to mark German industrial targets for the rest of the heavy bomber force to follow.

Its wooden construction gave the Mosquito speed and the ability to fly at high altitude, but the aircraft of the Pathfinder force would arrive in advance of the main bomber force, making them the only target for 500 or 600 German anti-aircraft guns during their time over any large target. As the navigator in a Mosquito, John sat up front beside the pilot, unlike the 'Navs' in heavy bombers, who sat at a table a few feet behind the rest of the flight crew. Ebanks therefore had an unwanted front row view of the action, which included searchlights and heavy volumes of flak.

When John Ebanks joined 571 Squadron it was still forming and for a time he was the only non–commissioned officer on the station. He found himself stuck all alone in a large building reserved for NCO accommodation and he thought constantly of his home and family. John was a trim, good looking and intelligent man, smart in his RAF uniform and clearly proud of having been selected to serve, yet there was little of the warrior about him and he still said his prayers every night before bed as his parents had taught him. All the same, John Ebanks could occasionally be short-tempered and bellicose when the mood took him. In the main, he looked more like what he had once been, a lay preacher and school teacher, than what he now was, a man who would guide a stream of several hundred heavily laden bombers through fire and storm and the ever present threat of swooping enemy night fighters to blast away the centre of a German city.

John Blair's long and exhaustive training was also over and he was considered ready to join an operational squadron. His fear that the war would end before he got there had been unfounded. In fact, John Blair was about to take part in the most intense stage of Bomber Command's fight.

Blair's crew was posted to No. 102 (Ceylon) Squadron, based at Pocklington in Yorkshire. During the Second World War, this bomber squadron had also flown the twin engine Whitley, before converting to the Halifax II, which it would operate from 1942 to 1944. These were later upgraded to the Halifax III in 1944 and to the Halifax VI in early 1945. It was in the last two models that John would serve during his tour of duty.

The squadron was very cosmopolitan, comprising men from Great Britain, Canada, Ceylon, the Caribbean, Australia and New Zealand, amongst others, and from all walks of life. Teachers, engineers, former policemen, clerks, professors and career RAF fliers all lived and worked together, sharing danger, friendship and beer with types and races they would never otherwise have come to know.

The squadron history reveals that 102 Squadron saw non–stop action over Europe from 1939 to 1945 and in 1944 the squadron flew its highest number of operational missions. The squadron supported the D-Day landings in Normandy in June 1944, bombing a coastal gun battery that could have opposed the Allied operation. Other major targets during the war included Berlin, Cologne, Frankfurt, Hamburg, Munich, and the Ruhr industrial area, Turin, Genoa and Milan, all of which were struck from its base in Yorkshire.

Following a further short familiarization course on the Halifax III, as their assigned aircraft at RAF Ricall, John Blair and the rest of his new crew arrived at their operational squadron in December 1944. So, this was it, John thought. Their operational Halifax III bomber, NA 615 'Z', was even more sophisticated than the one on which they had done their most recent familiarization training. Prior to being assigned to No. 102 Squadron, this particular aircraft had been flown by a French Squadron, No. 346, based at RAF Elvington, which collectively with RAF Melbourne and RAF Pocklington, was known as '42 Base'.

The crew's first flight was a bombing exercise and they also did some cross-country flying to ensure that they were familiar with the lie of the land around their airfield. The crew was complete by now and a good crew it was too, with their Canadian pilot Ralph Pearson, Jamaican navigator John Blair, three English air gunners, Sergeants G. Brown, J. Middleton and J. B. Lewis, a Scottish wireless operator, Sergeant T. W. Johnson, an English flight engineer from Liverpool, Sergeant L. J. Wylie and a Canadian bomb aimer, Sergeant A. Leslie. They were now thrown into the thick of the air war with little more than, 'There's your plane, there's the target, now get on with it'! Within three weeks of the new crew's arrival, 102 Squadron had lost another eight aircraft, or one third of its strength. Six of these Halifax aircraft went down over Germany.

Chapter 5

The Air War

They operated some of the most modern and sophisticated machines of war ever before seen. Although many different types and classes of aircraft were flown by Bomber Command, the mainstays of the night bombing campaign over Germany from 1943 onward, when most of the Caribbean volunteers were involved, were the twin engine Mosquito fighter-bomber and the Halifax and Lancaster four engine heavy bombers. Together, these last two bore the brunt of the long-range flying and fighting, and their crews suffered the heaviest losses.

The Lancaster was the main RAF heavy bomber by a small margin. It had the advantage of a long and unobstructed bomb bay, which allowed it to carry the largest and heaviest bombs then available. The Lancaster was developed after its predecessor, the twin engine Manchester, proved a failure. The factory added two more engines, redesigned the tail and the most successful RAF bomber of the war was born.

The Halifax could carry fewer bombs than the Lancaster and it also suffered heavier losses, making it statistically inferior in terms of the number of bombs dropped per airman killed. It was, however, a very important contributor to the campaign and it flew in large numbers throughout the war, with over 6,000 being built. The Halifax flew its first bombing mission to Le Havre on the night of 11 March 1941, a year before the Lancaster came into service, and this period was one of the most critical and costly in the bombing campaign.

Halifax crews loved their aircraft and often cited its advantages over the more prestigious Lancaster. Both aircraft could climb equally fast and high, but perhaps more importantly, it was easier to escape from a Halifax, than from a Lancaster, in an emergency. The Halifax had a wider body with more room to move and the escape hatch was in the floor near the pilot's feet and larger than the hatch in the Lancaster, which could seriously hinder men trying to escape the latter. In a burning aircraft falling toward the ground, such seemingly minor contrasts made the difference between life and death, as Bomber Command crews had only a one-in-ten chance overall of successfully bailing out from a stricken aircraft, although in the case of Halifax crews the survival rate was about twice as high.

John Ebanks and his pilot were part of a force of Pathfinders sent to mark the target at Cologne for a raid on the night of Thursday, 21 December 1944. Their aiming point was the main rail marshalling yard and it was attacked by a total of sixty-seven aircraft. The city was defended by hundreds of guns and the Mosquitos left the area weaving and turning violently to avoid the enemy fire. Looking back over his shoulder, John saw one remaining aircraft circling the target, apparently taking a closer look. It turned out to be one of the squadron leaders who was later shot down and killed doing the same thing over another target. John Blair and his crew took off for their first live action on this night, also bound for Cologne in the stream of bombers travelling in the wake of John Ebanks and the other Pathfinders. Classified as an industrial target, this city had already been heavily bombed by this stage of the war and much of it was in ruins.

To John Blair, the events before, during and immediately after his first mission were just a blur. He had been afraid of feeling fear, but when the time came he found that he had so much to do that he simply did not have time for feeling anything at all. He worked like a machine. John would experience this on all of the operational trips he made as he worked feverishly to make sure that the crew stayed within their group of bombers and that their timing was spot on. There was simply no room for error or for anything that could cause it.

During their briefing they had been told exactly when they needed to transit each waypoint along their assigned route, at what speed and at what altitude. With dozens, even hundreds of aircraft streaming toward the target, this was the only way to ensure that disastrous mid-air collisions between fully loaded four engine giants did not fill the sky. Collisions were nevertheless commonplace and they caused many casualties, as did prematurely detonating bomb loads. John had already been told by other crews about one recent case where a bomber exploded in mid-air and brought down three nearby aircraft with it.

The briefing was intended to be the first point in time when everyone in the crew knew with certainty what the target for that night would be. Many an educated guess would already have been made, based on the moon, weather, fuel load and type of bombs being loaded, as the identity and distance of the target determined the level of danger the men would be exposed to. Harry McCalla was renowned for being able to correctly predict the target without fail. His accuracy was so impressive that at one stage he was investigated to determine whether he was actually in receipt of leaked secret information from someone on the base. But Harry's instinct was apparently so powerful that he could even predict when a mission was about to be cancelled, and his crew mates learned to simply trust his judgement.

Today, we can barely imagine what the experience of setting off on such a mission must have been like. The crew had finished an intensive and extended period of training and they would have felt ready for this first operational flight, but climbing into a plane full of explosives in order to fly it towards hundreds of guns is not an easy thing to do, particularly when you know that the odds of surviving a full tour of thirty missions are close to zero. This was very hard indeed and as the men approached the aircraft they would have felt as though they were walking through treacle. Earlier that morning they had first been told that they were scheduled to fly later the same day. 'On duty tonight', was the terse command. They were given this warning at about ten o'clock in the morning and the mission took place between ten that night and two o'clock the following morning. The men had twelve hours to get ready and then a four hour period in which they had to complete the course to the target, drop their bombs and get back to their airfield in one piece.

As the navigator, John Blair had a lot of extra work to do in the time remaining before take-off. They ate lunch as a group, stodgy pies, spam, corned beef, boiled potatoes and over-cooked vegetables being standard fare and then, clutching their charts, the navigators from each squadron headed off to their separate briefing. Here they were told the identity of that night's target and the track to be flown. Most of the crew were still in the dark and did not yet know where they were headed, so they had more time to ponder their fate and to think about home and loved ones. Those with too vivid imaginations might dream up all the ways in which they could be dismembered, burned, disfigured or thrown into the night sky. While they were doing this, the 'Navs' took out their maps and drew in the route.

During the briefing the navigators sat on hard wooden chairs facing a large map of Europe mounted on the wall above a low stage. Covered by a curtain which would be pulled back during the briefing, the map was marked with tapes held in place by pins that showed the target for tonight and the bomber routes to and from the target. The route to each target was a zigzag course designed to confuse the enemy ground controllers. It was made up of a series of 'dog legs', each one taking them towards a waypoint and then going in a different direction. If the bombers had flown straight to their targets, the enemy would have guessed their destination easily and the night fighters would be ready and waiting. The routes were also designed to ensure that the bombers avoided the heaviest concentrations of anti-aircraft artillery fire, known as 'flak'.

Other considerations also affected the choice of both target and route. Targets were classified based on their strategic value, for example; oil targets, industrial, chemical, munitions, transport centres or worker's housing. In reality, the aiming point for night bombing was often just the city centre, but this did not change the practice of describing each target in strategic terms, an important psychological tool for dealing with many crews' natural reluctance to deliberately bomb civilian areas.

The time of year, weather and state of the moon were also of critical importance. Summer nights being shorter, the bombers could not be assigned targets deep inside Germany during that season, as they would lose the cover of darkness for much of their journey. Too much cloud would conceal the target, while too little would expose the bombers to heavier fire from the ground. A good moon could aid navigation and accuracy, especially over complex targets like the Ruhr, but moonlight also made the enemy night fighter's jobs much easier. And, of course, the amount of damage already caused to each target reduced its value in the eyes of planners, so that, as the war dragged on, the choice of targets decreased and the raids become ever more predictable.

The identification numbers of the squadron's aircraft and the names of their crews were chalked up on a blackboard. After most missions, one or two of these would be rubbed out and replaced, the only official acknowledgment of the ceaseless drain of human casualties and destroyed planes. This was just one marker of the relentless and unforgiving determination of Bomber Command's campaign. Another was the trail of death and destruction it left on the ground. It seemed that no defence, however fanatical, no amount of anti-aircraft fire, no volume of fighter intercepts, no number of highly skilled Nachtjager pilots, could turn back the tide. Night after night, over city after city, the bomber streams came on, raining their high explosives and incendiaries upon the hapless population below. Two hundred, five hundred, a thousand aircraft in columns many miles long, the droning lumbering machines would fly in and drop their bombs onto their targets, seemingly oblivious to the storm of flak from hundreds of German heavy guns, or the huge mid-air explosions as one or more of their fellows was hit.

On the walk to the aircraft for his first operational flight, many a man felt as though he was moving in slow motion and that his legs did not want to carry him. Some recalled that rather than feeling fear they were unusually aware of their immediate surroundings and completely focused on the task at hand, to the exclusion of all other thoughts. For most, the time for thinking was past and it was now time for action.

After the war, Miles Tripp asked his Jamaican rear gunner, Harry McCalla, if the fear that they had shared during their tour had affected him psychologically afterwards. 'No', replied Harry. But what about his stomach pains? Harry hadn't even been able to take a drink because of them. 'That was down to the food,' Harry told Miles, 'all that Spam and potatoes!'

Each navigator would sit at his little table in the depths of the bomber with his navigational aids and charts laid out before him, listening to the chatter on the intercom as the pilot went through the familiar procedures for take-off. 'Heaters on. Trim tabs on. Elevator set. Master fuel cocks on. Selector cocks to No. 2 tank. Booster pumps set. Radiator flaps open. Flaps at 15 degrees. Ignition.' The engines would thunder into life, one by one, and then each aircraft would trundle heavily across the airfield towards the runway. A brief pause as they lined up and the pilot pushing the throttles all the way forward took the aircraft into a swinging, vibrating, bumping, thundering run down the runway, approaching the take-off speed of 105 miles per hour with painful slowness, then heaving back on the controls with all of his two-handed strength while the flight engineer leaned over to maintain the throttle position. Suddenly, the vibration diminished and the undercarriage came up with a distinct 'thunk'. Ever so slowly now, foot by foot, the huge bird would claw its way into the air, its wheels still spinning as they left the earth, the four great engines dragging the plane, its 8,000lbs of explosives, 2,000 gallons of fuel and 1,200lbs of human flesh ever higher into the freezing night sky.

These lumbering aircraft were mechanical marvels, built by hand in huge numbers, each plane containing over 50,000 separate parts. The flight engineer was responsible for most technical matters affecting the aircraft during flight, with the exception of the guns and bombs. Often coming from a background in industry or the automotive trade, he was typically a hands-on practical type who knew the aircraft inside out and was capable of fixing almost anything while flying at 20,000 feet, possibly under fire, with only a limited toolset available. The flight engineer gave technical guidance to the pilot in addition to helping him operate the controls during take-off and landing. He kept constant watch on the gauges that displayed fuel states, oil and engine temperatures, and looked after the hydraulics, mechanical controls, and numerous sensitive pieces of technical equipment, as well as the oxygen supplies.

Levelling out after their climb, the engines now synchronized and emitting a steady drone, the bomber would form up with the rest of the squadron as the whole unit made its first turn and headed off towards the east, glimmers of moonlight allowing them to distinguish between sky, land and sea. They had merely completed the opening act. It was when they crossed the English coastline and headed towards the coast of Holland that the real action would begin. John Blair recalled staring out at the dark landscape below and secretly wondering once again what he was doing here, a black man from Jamaica on his way to bomb Nazi Germany.

By this time, Flight Sergeant Lincoln Orville Lynch, also of Jamaica and serving in 102 (Ceylon) Squadron, was already a veteran air gunner, hunched behind the tail guns of his Halifax. Alone at the rear of the aircraft, he had a more limited field of view than the mid-upper turret gunner. The tail gunner's mount was a sophisticated cylindrical device that protruded from the rear of the aircraft. Orville Lynch could move the guns up and down freely and also swivel them left and right, but to a more limited extent. The two gunners had a different perspective, as the mid-upper turret gunner had his head protruding from the top of the aircraft, protected from the elements by a perspex cone. He would be constantly revolving his turret throughout the flight, scanning a full circle for any sign of enemy aircraft above or alongside the bomber.

Lynch never forgot his first operational flight. Two years of training and preparation had taken him to this place, high in the night skies, staring out into the blackness, his eyes peeled for any indication of a presence that did not belong. He would remain like this for several hours, the sea or land receding in front of him as he flew backwards all the way to the target and back. He was cramped and motionless, the bitter cold seeping in through any gaps in his covering, his responsibility for the safety of the rest of the crew uppermost in his mind. A tail gunner who daydreamed was a tail gunner who died, often along with his crew.

The risks grew as they approached the German frontier. Searchlights stabbed the darkness and flak explosions pulsed red and orange at various points. Occasionally, the sky would be lit by the huge flash of an exploding bomber, or a funeral pyre would glimmer far below on the ground, its light visible to Lynch for many minutes after they had passed over it. He knew that there, but for the grace of God, he would go too.

Suddenly, Lynch was aware of something lurking, a blacker section of sky against the backdrop of the night. It was too big to be his imagination but too small to be another heavy bomber. Lynch could just make out the conical nose and twin engines of a German night fighter, looking as though it had come straight from one of his aircraft recognition manuals, or from the many posters pinned up around the squadron's base.

This was the aerial equivalent of the gunfights all boys of Lynch's generation had watched in the American cowboy movies of his childhood, and even of his adulthood. The difference here was that it was Lynch himself facing a terribly efficient foe in the dusty street and both men were armed with heavy machine guns or cannons capable of blowing the other's whole aircraft into oblivion. All the same, like a western gunfight, this too would come down to who could shoot first and most accurately.

Orville Lynch had no time to think about the philosophical framework in which he was trapped. Without hesitating, and without taking the time to warn his pilot, he swung his four gun barrels towards the enemy night fighter and fired. The rounds slammed home and one of the fighters' engines immediately caught fire. The German pilot opened his canopy and both crewmen, pilot and rear gunner, started to climb out. Fascinated by the sight, Lynch held his fire and watched the men. Aware that they should have already received a second volley, but that it had not yet come, the Germans glanced towards the British bomber. Then they leapt from their crippled aircraft and disappeared into the night.

The German fighter was still flying straight and level, about 200 yards away, now burning fiercely. With its crew gone, Lynch took his time, aimed carefully and fired long bursts into the dying bird. After a few seconds it rolled over into a vertical dive, heading for the hard earth below. Lynch watched it go until it was hidden by cloud. He had shot down a German aircraft on his very first mission and he would later receive the DFM for his conduct.

The tail gunners had perhaps the least enviable role of anyone aboard. Unable to move and with nothing to protect them from enemy fire, they spent the mission flying backwards, staring out into the inky darkness in an attempt to spot enemy night fighters. When they did, they would generally call out a warning and the pilot would make the limited evasive manoeuvres permitted by the circumstances. If they were in the bomber stream, their movement was very constrained. Turning left or right could prove fatal. However, the main dangers were tiredness and boredom. On an eight hour trip it was entirely possible that nothing would be spotted and other than the fires burning at the target, which the tail gunner would see last as the aircraft headed home, the black wall of the night might be the only thing he saw. Staying awake, much less staying alert, was a serious challenge.

The gunners were also responsible for the care and maintenance of their guns. Lincoln Lynch was already the holder of the RAF Air Gunner's trophy of 1944 and a proven expert in the use and upkeep of his four Browning machine guns. Many tail gunners were killed during the war and it was not unknown for the whole tail gun assembly to be shot off with the gunner still in it, the aircraft returning home without him. This was a hard way to go and there was no chance to bail out of an amputated tail turret as it spun rapidly to earth.

The Final Prayer
Mark Johnson, 2013

The boom and the crack
The cannon's loud roar
Their cymbals of flak
An orchestra of war

Their sirens below
Our four engine rhythm
Conducted by searchlights
This fiery bright mayhem

That beat of the drum
Is the beat of my heart
My time has now come
Our Father, who art...

The majority of the German night fighters were actually modified fighter-bomber and light bomber aircraft that were no longer effective in daylight. These twin-engine planes had been fitted with radar and extra armaments to enable them to find and destroy Allied bombers in the dark. The crews were specialists who flew only at night and they belonged to elite 'Nachtjagd' or night fighter units. They were also guided onto their targets by radar equipped flight controllers working on the ground, but the radar system was not accurate enough to take the fighters all the way to their targets.

Once in the vicinity of the British bombers, the German night fighter pilots had to grope their way forward in the blackness, as much at risk of collision as their opponents. This meant that when fire was exchanged it often happened at very close range, sometimes less than 100 metres. Often, as we saw with Lynch, two men stared at each other in surprise down the sights of their cannons and machine guns and then blazed away at one another, the quickest and most accurate living to tell the tale, the other falling 20,000 feet to be smashed to pieces or swallowed by the sea. The tail gunner was therefore critical to the bombers' defence.

As the war progressed, German night fighter pilots would more commonly attack a bomber from below, because that was their blind spot and the attacker therefore stood much less chance of being detected and fired upon. By now, the German aircraft had special gun mountings, fitted to point upwards to support this direction of attack, in a configuration the Germans called 'Schräge Musik' or Jazz Music. The Luftwaffe also had the world's first jet fighters in the air, although these only flew by day. John Blair described them as being 'as quick as the devil'.

Flying and correctly navigating a heavily loaded bomber in congested airspace, with few of today's electronic tools, required real skill and was physically demanding, as the aircraft lacked the vast array of gauges and instruments that modern bombers possess. This could degenerate into real 'seat of your pants' flying in an emergency. In the cockpit the pilot had an altimeter, showing the aircraft's height above sea level, a tachometer displaying their airspeed, an attitude indicator that indicated the angle of the aircraft relative to the horizon, RPM indicators for each of the four engines, a compass and a few other dials for fuel state, oil pressure and engine temperature.

Much of the time, the navigator couldn't see a great deal, other than his maps and instruments, the drone of the engines and the occasional comments from the other members of the crew on the intercom being his only contact with the world beyond his cubicle. Idle chatter was strongly discouraged, as the channel needed to be kept open in case one of the crew spotted some danger. John Blair sat at his table, alone with his charts and separated from the others by a curtain that hid the lights he needed for map-reading from any nearby enemy night fighter. He used a red light to read the maps as the enemy fighter pilots were constantly on the lookout for any little flash of light in the black sky, whether from a torch, a spark from an engine, or the glint of the moon on perspex or metal.

For most of the journey, John Blair had his head down over his charts and instruments, working hard to keep his pilot on track. In addition to a small pile of maps and other papers, as well as familiar tools such as protractors, rulers and coloured pencils, he also had repeats of the altimeter, airspeed indicator and the compass that the pilot saw. Periodically he would get up from his desk and take a quick look outside to check what the weather was doing, for this could push them off course, and also to get a fix on their position over the ground if it was visible. When they were over the target he could not see the effect of the bombs or the flak that was exploding outside the aircraft; his work was to guide the pilot to the target and then home again, not to sightsee.

Aside from collisions, another frequent cause of death was bombs falling on an aircraft from one above, neither crew being aware of the other's presence. Frank de Verteuil of Trinidad, whose family provided no less than ten RAF volunteers, comments:

'Suddenly the mid upper gunner shouted, "Gee, what's going on?" I looked up and saw the plane above us dropping bombs, which fell on either side of us. We must have said our prayers good that morning.'

Sitting in the tail of his aircraft, Jamaican Harry McCalla saw two Lancasters explode simultaneously when bombs landed on them, dropped by an aircraft above them in the bomber stream. He reported it over the intercom. A few seconds later another crewman called out, 'There goes another, Harry', making it three aircraft in total, but the third was outside Harry's field of view.

The men knew that they were as likely to be killed by their own side as they were by the enemy and the job would have been hair-raisingly dangerous even if the enemy had held their fire throughout. Cold and the weather were equally formidable foes. McCalla suffered frostbite on a raid conducted at altitude and he had to knock ice off his oxygen mask and helmet when the aircraft landed.

As the planes approached the enemy coast the first things the crew saw were the searchlights. They knew that German night fighters were also out there in the dark looking for them. As they neared Cologne there were more searchlights and lots of flak over the target. The actual bombing run – the last leg leading in to the target – only took about ten minutes between the time they turned onto it and the time they released their bombs. When the bombs fell from the bomb bay in the belly of the aircraft, the plane leapt upwards and John Blair felt his heart leap upwards as well, for he was happy to be rid of all that high explosive, a sentiment shared by all on board. After the bombs were safely away the pilot twisted and turned as they left the target area in case there were enemy fighter aircraft waiting to hit them on the way out, taking advantage of the light from the fires below. Then they pointed their nose in the direction of home, heading once more into darkness, back to their base away over the sea. Behind them the fires blazed and the tail gunners stared out at a sea of burning buildings and tornadoes of black smoke.

It was only when they had cleared the target and left behind the zone where they could most expect to meet enemy night fighters that John allowed himself to relax slightly. Dangers still lay ahead, but the bombs were gone and the worst of the flak was behind them. The enemy gunners were shooting at other inbound aircraft now and the immense pressure that was caused by the combination of fear, stress and fatigue had lifted.

On this first night, the rail yards they had attacked had been targeted because they were being used to support the final unsuccessful German western offensive in the Ardennes. No aircraft were lost during this mission, but as the target was cloud-covered, only a few bombs actually hit the railway yards.

Although he flew in 1943, Cy Grant's experience of his first operation was almost identical to that recounted by John Blair:

'As navigator, one was kept continuously occupied. You did not see much of what was going on below. It may have been completely different for my pilot, having to fly the Lancaster through all that flak, or for the gunners looking out for fighters, or indeed for all the other members of the crew. For myself, my sense of responsibility for getting us there and back was paramount, and that may be why the obvious danger of the situation did not seem to get to me ... In any event, whenever I had a peek, and that was only when we were over the target (the bomb aimer directs the course of the aircraft during these few minutes), I was only too happy to get back to my station to work out a course that would get us away from the scene; away from the noise of the battle, the flares, the searchlights, the inferno below, and the unnerving jolting of the aircraft.

'Even amidst the deafening drone of scores of other aircraft, the muffled explosions below, the glow of the target area, the flak, the sweeping searchlights and the sudden bumps as the aircraft rode the frenzied skies, I never questioned what I was doing there. I cannot remember feeling particularly frightened; the thought of death did not cross my mind. It was as though we were in another state of consciousness, emotionally switched off, yet our minds functioning clearly as we got on with the things we each had to do.'

Despite John Blair's loss-free start, the generally unremitting death toll was grim. Three days after their first operational flight, on Christmas Eve 1944, the crew set out on their second operation, this time to bomb Mülheim as part of a force of 338 aircraft, twenty-four of which were provided by 102 Squadron. Described as 'Ops II' in John Blair's logbook, this time there were bags of flak waiting for the bombers and the attack was described as a 'complete hang up', a nasty business. The aircraft were attacking the airfields at Lohausen and Mülheim (now Düsseldorf and Essen civil airports). One squadron aircraft, Halifax MZ871DY-G, was hit and crashed near Neuss, Germany. The two air gunners, James 'Lofty' Williams and John Simpson, aged twenty-three and thirty-seven respectively, were killed in the crash, while the rest of the crew parachuted to safety and were taken prisoner. A second bomber from the squadron also went down, hit by flak and crashing near Krefeld, with its 29-year-old pilot, Edward Hislop and 22-year-old bomb aimer Kevin Lindenboom both killed and the other five again being taken prisoner. One more Halifax from another squadron was also shot down during the attack, but visibility was good and despite the losses, the bombing was described as 'accurate and effective'.

Contrary to popular perceptions in Britain and America at the time, the term 'precision bombing' was a misnomer when applied to the heavy bomber force, as bombing by all nations engaged in the conflict was often wildly inaccurate. Merely hitting the centre of a large city could prove difficult enough for the average Bomber Command crew and bombing a particular factory or a ship was a task best suited to only the most highly trained fliers. Accuracy for Bomber Command night raiders depended on several factors. Firstly, the expert Pathfinders who preceded the main force had to identify the target correctly in the dark and often through cloud, while they themselves were also the only target available for hundreds of enemy flak gunners on the ground and night fighters in the air. Secondly, the Pathfinders had to mark the target accurately, either by bombing it themselves with pyrotechnic coloured flares, or by using sky marker flares that floated above the clouds over the target when conditions made this necessary. Thirdly, the main bomber force had to find the target area, locate the markers and drop their bombs accurately on those markers.

Pathfinder accuracy itself faced a number of challenges. The first Pathfinders to arrive and mark the target had to get this right, because experience showed that even follow-on Pathfinder crews would often ignore what their own instruments and navigation were telling them and drop their own markers on top of those already visible, compounding any errors made by the early arrivals. The wind was also an important factor for all bombing, with strong gusts sometimes blowing bombs off target and frequently blowing sky markers away from the point at which they had been dropped. This could lead to the follow-on Pathfinders and the main force bombing the wrong parts of a city, or, and this was commonplace, dropping their loads into open country. Even when bombing was accurate, more than thirty per cent of bombs dropped overall by Bomber Command during the campaign are thought to have failed to explode.

The Germans were very familiar with bomber tactics, having developed many of these themselves during their earlier bombing campaigns. In fact, the RAF had adopted and adapted Luftwaffe tactics at all levels as it evolved its own fighter and bomber strategies. The Germans would light dummy target markers in open country to deceive the Bomber Command fliers and this technique was often effective.

The RAF introduced continual improvements, including the use of a Master Bomber, an expert crew that would coordinate the actions of the remainder of the force as it arrived in a stream, as well as more reliable and more powerful bombs, improved electronic navigation aids and better bomb sights. As a result, Bomber Command's accuracy continued to improve and by 1944 effective attacks against small targets such as rail yards and U-boat pens were not only feasible, but commonplace. A part of this success, exemplified by the attack on the German battleship *Tirpitz*, arose from the use of much bigger bombs that had a greatly enhanced chance of destroying a target, even if they fell a short distance away. *Tirpitz* was hit by a 12,000lb 'Tallboy' bomb, specially designed for such raids. Nonetheless, the combined effects of the difficulties of bombing accurately – which never really went away even in perfect conditions – crew errors, hesitation on the part of some crews to bomb heavily defended targets, or civilian areas already on fire, and enemy deceptions meant that anything from ten per cent to fifty per cent of bombs on target was considered both normal and acceptable. The remainder of the bombs dropped, representing thousands of tons of high explosives, were expected to fall randomly at all points of the compass.

As John Blair reported it, based on his tour between December 1944 and March 1945:

'The massive quantities of bombs that we carried and dropped on a target were bound to cause large numbers of casualties on the ground. You would try your hardest to navigate accurately and to bomb with precision, but you could never be right on target every time. You would think you had the right wind direction, and the right wind speed, and that there would not be a deviation between the wind at your height and the wind on the ground, but at the end of the day, if you're dropping that kind of weaponry from that sort of height, you know that you're going to wipe out whatever is on the ground below you. Remember, we were bombing from 20,000 feet, which meant that there were miles of air beneath us, with winds blowing this way and that, and we were unable to measure and adapt to those deviations.

'On many occasions we were confident that we had the aircraft perfectly aligned, just as it should be. The bomb aimer had his sights on the target, all his calculations had been completed and the aircraft was ready for a perfect bomb run, but when he released the bombs they just did not fall where he intended because of a wind shear somewhere beneath us. The wind would just take the bombs off target and they would land some distance away, often on civilian areas that were not being targeted. You would do your best, but there were just too many factors to take into account, many of them out of your control. That's the nature of the beast. You tried your best.'

Five days after the Mülheim raid, another squadron aircraft, Halifax MZ426DY-D, was damaged during a raid to Koblenz, with one crewman wounded, and on 1 January 1945, yet another plane returning from Dortmund undershot on landing. The bomb aimer, James Sheridan, died, while five of the crew were injured. The following day, Halifax NR186 overshot during training and crashed. This time the crew were unharmed.

Then, on the night of 5/6 January, disaster really struck. No. 102 Squadron had committed twenty aircraft to a force attacking the city of Hannover. They were part of a total of 664 bombers, including 340 Halifax, 310 Lancaster, and fourteen Mosquito bombers acting as Pathfinders. This was the first large raid against the city since October 1943 and the aim was to complete the destruction wrought by that earlier mission. There was cloud over the target, so the Master Bomber in his Mosquito dropped sky markers and the bombers then proceeded to drop their loads as ordered. The glow of fires could be seen through the clouds.

German opposition over Hannover was more intense than it had been of late and numerous night fighter flares were seen by the bomber crews. These flares were used by the night fighters to spot the British aircraft in the dark. A total of twenty-three Halifaxs and eight Lancasters were lost, thirty-one bombers in all, representing 4.7 per cent of the attacking force. Three of the Halifaxs were 102 Squadron bombers, shot down over the target. Five crewmen were killed and two taken prisoner from each of the first two aircraft, while the entire crew of the third Halifax was killed in their crash.

The same thing happened again on 16 January, when the entire crew of Halifax LW179DY-Y was killed after their aircraft was shot down on a mission to Magdeburg. John Blair's crew took part in each of these operations and the lost aircraft were snatched from the air around them as they made their way to their targets. By now, John and his crew were already veterans and new crews of green recruits were arriving daily, as were new aircraft, to fill the spaces left by those shot down.

Some men found themselves unable to continue in the face of almost certain death. In 1941, Billy Strachan had joined a squadron of Wellington bombers and was making almost nightly raids over heavily defended German cities as a sergeant wireless operator/air gunner with 99 Squadron, based at Waterbeach in Cambridgeshire. Having somehow survived the mandatory first tour of thirty operations over enemy territory, he was now due a period of rest before starting his final tour of twenty missions. But Strachan was still eager for more and he requested retraining as a pilot. He learned quickly and was allowed to fly solo with only seven hours flight time in his logbook. As Strachan described it:

'We had the overconfidence of youth. We never thought it would happen to us. As a crew, we did everything together. At the end of a raid we came back, had parties, checked up to see who had been lost and heartlessly said things like, "Oh, I'll have his girlfriend, or his bike, if he isn't coming back".'

In 1942, Billy Strachan became a bomber pilot with 101 Squadron, fulfilling his life's dream. Pilot Officer Strachan was infamous for waiting until the enemy was right on his tail and then, at the last minute, sending his aircraft into a plunging dive, letting the fighter overshoot. Strachan gained two more promotions to become first a Flying Officer and then a Flight Lieutenant, but on his fifteenth trip as a pilot, three quarters of the way through his second tour, his nerve finally snapped. He gave a Press interview after the war:

'I remember so clearly. I was carrying a 12,000lb Blockbuster bomb destined for some German shipping. We were stationed in Lincolnshire and our flight path was over Lincoln Cathedral. It was a foggy night, with visibility about 100 yards (90 metres). I asked my engineer, who stood beside me, to make sure we were on course to get over the top of the cathedral tower. He replied, "We've just passed it." I looked out and suddenly realized that it was just beyond our wingtips, to the side. This was the last straw. It was sheer luck. I hadn't seen it at all – and I was the pilot! There and then my nerve went. I knew I simply couldn't go on – that this was the end of me as a pilot! I flew to a special "hole" we had in the North Sea, which no allied shipping ever went near, and dropped my "big one". Then I flew back to the airfield.'

After this incident, Strachan was assigned to train pilots for the Pathfinder Force with 156 Squadron. As a stark reminder of the dangers faced even during training, Billy's close friend Roy Ashman was a fighter pilot who survived the war and was then killed shortly afterward when a Hurricane fighter he was transporting from one airfield to another exploded in mid-air.

Chapter 6

The Bombs

'... we can see that the temperatures must have ranged between 1300 to 1400 degrees Celsius and the area lacked oxygen ... Above ground the temperatures must have been even higher (perhaps) as high as 1600 degrees Celsius ... Human beings were transformed into ashes.'

Berlin Archaeologist Uwe Mueller
on the Allied bombing of Dresden

The bombs they dropped were designed for many different purposes and targets. High explosive bombs, or 'HE', could rip open buildings, exposing the interiors and they could also knock down or shatter concrete walls and neutralize any firebreaks that might otherwise impede the progress of a fire. By dropping HE mixed with incendiaries containing phosphorous, which burns on contact with the air, the chances of starting major fires that would rapidly take hold and spread were greatly improved. The HE would tear the buildings apart, so that the incendiaries could more readily ignite the flammable materials inside, such as carpeting, interior walls and wooden furniture. HE would also break gas lines, hugely increasing the chances of major fires erupting.

For some targets, such as oil production and storage facilities, where fires were likely to result from HE explosions alone, incendiaries were not used, or they were used in smaller quantities. On highly flammable targets, Japanese cities being the prime example, raids might be conducted with incendiaries alone, these missions being referred to as 'fire-bombing' raids. In every case, the primary aim was to trigger large, self-sustaining fires that would rapidly overwhelm the capacity for fire fighters to respond and this would lead to the greatest possible destruction of infrastructure and loss of life.

Often, a gap in the bombing would follow the first attack, during which it was hoped that fire and other emergency workers would rush to the scene. Thirty minutes later another wave of bombers would drop more HE to kill the rescue teams, police and any survivors who had emerged from shelters. Bombs with deliberately delayed fuses would also be dropped, sometimes one per aircraft. These would explode unpredictably over a period of many hours, again frustrating fire fighting and rescue efforts, while inflicting further casualties.

Lothar Metzger, Dresden survivor:

'It is not possible to describe! Explosion after explosion. It was beyond belief, worse than the blackest nightmare. So many people were horribly burnt and injured. It became more and more difficult to breathe. It was dark and all of us tried to leave this cellar with inconceivable panic. Dead and dying people were trampled upon, luggage was left, or snatched up out of our hands by rescuers. The basket, with our twins covered with wet cloths, was snatched up out of my mother's hands and we were pushed upstairs by the people behind us. We saw the burning street, the falling ruins and the terrible firestorm. My mother covered us with wet blankets and coats she found in a water tub.

'We saw terrible things: cremated adults shrunk to the size of small children, pieces of arms and legs, dead people, whole families burnt to death, burning people ran to and fro, burnt coaches filled with civilian refugees, dead rescuers and soldiers, many were calling and looking for their children and families, and fire everywhere, everywhere fire, and all the time the hot wind of the firestorm threw people back into the burning houses they were trying to escape from.

'I cannot forget these terrible details. I can never forget them.'

The raging fires which, given a decent wind, could coalesce into thousand degree firestorms, would engulf whole city sections, burning human beings to charred cinders, dotting the molten asphalt streets with additional pools of burning, bubbling human fat and killing thousands of people in a single attack. An effective firestorm, carefully planned and efficiently triggered, could annihilate as many people as the initial explosion of an atomic bomb. For example, bombing attacks by the RAF and the USAAF on Hamburg in July 1943 created one of the largest firestorms seen during the war, killing more than 42,000 people and injuring another 37,000. The area destroyed was estimated to be four times larger than that destroyed by the atomic bombs dropped two years later on Hiroshima and Nagasaki, where an estimated 45,000 and 30,000 died respectively as a direct result of those explosions, although it should be noted that acute effects more than doubled the number of atomic bomb victims over a subsequent period of two to three months.

High explosive bombs came in various sizes, again with different purposes. The 250lb General Purpose bomb was the mainstay of the Allied air forces, but it lacked penetrating power and a significant proportion of the General Purpose bombs dropped failed to explode. Heavy bunkers and U-boat pens, which were encased in layers of concrete and steel several metres thick, were in any case generally impervious to such weapons. Much larger 4,000lb Blockbuster bombs, colloquially known by the crews as 'cookies', were developed by the RAF as a response. These were so heavy that each four engine bomber could only carry one, usually along with clusters of incendiaries and a few smaller high explosive bombs. Although originally intended to be dropped onto military defences, the cookie was soon employed in attacks on cities, where its massive blast effects proved highly efficient at ripping buildings apart for the incendiaries to then do their work. The blast from a cookie was so intense that any aircraft dropping even the smallest version from a height of less than 5,000 feet, risked being damaged or destroyed by the force of the resulting explosion.

As the war progressed, the Blockbuster bombs, which looked like heavy metal tubes about the diameter of a home garbage can rather than like typical aerial bombs, became longer and longer. An 8,000lb version was created by joining two 4,000lb bombs together end-to-end and eventually another 4,000lb section was added to create a 12,000lb weapon of massive destructive power. Nothing like this had ever existed before. These gargantuan containers of high explosives would be dropped onto German cities by the thousand, with the first 'cookie' being dropped on Berlin as early as 1943. Ultimately, a 22,000lb Grand Slam earthquake bomb was designed by

British inventor Barnes Wallis. Earthquake bombs were eventually used for a variety of difficult targets, the most impressive being a section of French railway track in a tunnel under a mountain. A Grand Slam was dropped, it drilled through several yards of solid rock and then destroyed the tunnel near Saumur, preventing German reinforcements from reaching the D-Day beaches in Normandy. The damage was not repaired until after the war.

The incendiaries represented another smorgasbord of death-dealing devices, with the size, filling, and design of each bomb used being determined by the details of the target. In addition to the phosphorus bombs, there were larger 250lb liquid fire bombs, containing a mixture of fuel and rubber for spreading fire over a wide area, while smaller magnesium incendiary 'stick bombs', weighing only 4lbs, were packed together in batches of 236 in a single case and also scattered by the thousand. A 30lb version of the stick bomb was widely used, packed together in batches of twenty-four. These small bombs would start numerous separate fires, often at roof level, and while each fire was initially small, they were harder for fire crews to spot and extinguish before they took hold because of their location. Allied incendiaries were very similar to the incendiaries dropped on London and other cities by the Luftwaffe from late 1940 onward, from which lessons had been learned, and the Allied versions were equally effective.

Penetrating incendiary bombs were soon developed to crash through to the interior of a large structure before exploding in a mass of flame inside the building. All across the Allied world, many of the best scientific minds of the age were focused exclusively on the challenge of bringing the maximum explosive force to bear on the largest possible numbers of citizens in enemy nations. When backed up by British and American industrial supremacy, the implications of these scientific advancements for the peoples of Germany and Japan were terrifying.

Carrying such large amounts of explosives to any target, or merely trying to load them onto an aircraft, had its own risks. Aircraft would sometimes explode prior to take-off, due to some fault with the device, or human error. On a regular basis planes would be hit in the bomb bay by flak while airborne, the resulting explosions creating miniature suns in the night sky that would temporarily blind other nearby crews and which could cause the destruction of other planes flying close to the victim. The implications for morale of these regular mid-air explosions were so serious that the RAF deliberately fabricated a tale for its crews of a new German secret weapon designed to flash in the night sky, giving the impression that an aircraft had exploded where none had been. This story was not widely believed and throughout the war bomber crews feared a mid-air collision between heavily loaded bombers, or the ignition of their own bomb load, even more than they feared enemy fighters or flak. After a successful enemy night fighter attack there was still the prospect of bailing out and landing by parachute, but a mid-air collision normally implied a huge fireball consuming all within it, the sky filled with falling embers and fragments of planes, whole engines, bits of men and bomb casings.

During the RAF attack on the medieval city of Dresden in February 1945, the 800 bombers involved dropped 650,000 incendiaries, along with hundreds of 8,000lb and 4,000lb blockbusters. The total dropped amounted to 2,600 tons of bombs. The resulting smoke from the fires rose to 15,000 feet and the glow of the flames that engulfed the city could be seen from the air 500 miles away. When American bombers arrived the following day to continue the attack, the previous night's fires were still blazing fiercely below them.

Many of the Allied crews had felt relief when Dresden had been announced as the target for that night. Although it represented the deepest penetration into Germany that most of them would make, a majority had never even heard of the city before and this meant that it was in all probability not a strategic target that would be heavily defended. In fact, Dresden's only real significance as a target was a product of recent military events on the ground. The Soviet advance was bringing the war ever closer to the heart of the Third Reich and Allied planners noted the fact that Dresden was a rail and road hub that they felt needed to be bombed heavily in order to hinder German troop movements.

The bombing would be carried out just seventy miles from the Russian front line and the bombers would take nine hours to travel the route to the target and back. The bomber stream for this raid was so extensive that, even with the long route to be travelled, some aircraft were still taking off in England while the foremost raiders were on the last leg of their approach to the target. On approaching the city, still more than forty miles out, flames were clearly visible to the follow-on crews. Six miles out and the crews could see a blazing latticework of streets and buildings. The other aircraft in the stream nearby were now brightly illuminated, not by searchlights, but by the flames below. The burning streets stretched east and west, north and south, in a saturation of flame and smoke that awed all who witnessed it. Some crews, recalling what they had witnessed themselves as victims of German bombing, deliberately turned away and dropped their bombs in what they hoped was open country, but many others pressed home their attacks.

According to the account of Miles Tripp, Harry McCalla's bomb aimer, his squadron had been briefed that Dresden's population was swollen by refugees fleeing the ravening Red Army and that this was designed to be a 'panic raid', as well as a raid on communications. Because the number of refugees present is not known with any degree of certainty and establishing the toll of the attack on those refugees is consequently impossible, it is also impossible to accurately calculate the total number of casualties caused by the British and American raids. Various estimates put the figure at between 25,000 and 100,000 civilians killed by blast, fire and suffocation in a twenty-four hour period and some revisionist German sources claim even higher numbers. It is very possible that Dresden represents the worst loss of life from a single aerial bombardment in history. British Prime Minister Winston Churchill, though doing nothing to interfere with Bomber Command's strategy at the time, later denounced the bombing of German cities as 'mere acts of terror and wanton destruction'.

Cy Grant:

'I don't think aircrew were fully conscious of the havoc and destruction they were causing. All they were thinking was "drop those bombs on the target and get out of there". Warfare denudes you of your humanity. Yes, I had sought adventure, an escape from a dull future in a British colony, but reflecting on it afterwards, I feel no sense of pride.'

As an economically dominant Germany has become more confident and assertive in recent years, those whose main response to Germany's Nazi past was contrition and shame are being replaced by other voices calling stridently for an Allied apology for what they term, 'The German Holocaust'. Some older Germans still refer to Allied aircrews as 'terror-fliers' and modern revisionist websites abound, some clearly neo-Nazi in character, others less easy to classify. It takes only a few minutes online to find images of large numbers of Germans marching today to protest at the bombing of Dresden, for example, or to locate well written articles describing the Germans as victims who had done nothing to deserve their punishment. There is certainly a real possibility that such revisionist sentiment will strengthen and that this is a conversation we will be forced to have with the Germans at some point, as unchallenged revisionist thinking poses a political threat to Europe at large and also to vulnerable segments of modern German society.

None of the objections to the Allied bombing campaign, whether voiced at the time, or now, change the simple fact that Europe had been a continent essentially at peace, until Nazi Germany launched its series of completely unprovoked attacks on its neighbours. The attacks were the follow-on to an already aggressive expansionist strategy, overlaid with an extreme racist ideology the likes of which had never been seen before. Nor do those objections change the grim reality of rape, exploitation, epic theft, persecution and genocide experienced by tens of millions of Europe's citizens under the Nazi heel. They do nothing to alter the statistic that twenty-five per cent of Germany's workforce in 1944 consisted of slave labour taken by the Nazi authorities to work in its fields and factories, or that one third of all the world's works of art were looted by the Nazis between 1939 and 1945. Germany, led by Hitler, but with a populace that was heavily complicit in his crimes, 'had sown the wind' and she would now 'reap the whirlwind'.

It is also a simple truth that many German soldiers of all branches were either silent witness to, or directly responsible for, the deaths of millions who should have been protected by them, including prisoners of war and innocent civilian victims, during the merciless and unprecedented racial war that was fought in the east. Even senior German officers wrote of their shame at what was taking place and predicted that their nation would one day be called to account for its actions. The German's slaughter, repression and grand larceny during a war that killed more people than any other in history, was sustained by Germany's cities, and by the factories and civilian workers within them, that produced the necessary guns, tanks, aircraft, submarines, uniforms, electronics, fuel, chemicals, electricity and all the other elements needed to maintain the engine of war.

Some sample statistics showing numbers killed during the Second World War in Europe sum up the tale.

Country	Population 1939**	Military deaths	Civilian deaths	Total deaths	Deaths as % of population
Germany*	69	5.5	3.5***	9	13
Poland	35	0.24	5	5.24	15
USSR	168	10	14	24	14

*   As defined by her 1937 borders.
**   All figures are in millions
***   Includes German victims of the Jewish Holocaust

What this simple table reveals is that Germany inflicted vastly disproportionate harm upon its neighbours while suffering a percentage loss (when its own victims of the Holocaust are included) that corresponds closely with that suffered by the other nations who suffered most heavily. Considering the USSR and Poland alone, Germany's main genocidal victims, the Germans inflicted almost thirty million deaths in comparison with a German total loss from all causes, and on all fronts, of nine million. When German Jews, other concentration camp victims and losses to Allied strategic bombing are removed, the German loss figure falls to perhaps seven or eight million, a ratio of three-to-one or better in her favour. This is not the profile of a victim.

There can simply be no disputing the notion that Germany's actions between 1939 and 1945 constitute the greatest war crime in human experience without avoiding, denying or altering the underlying facts. For all the passion I have found in the revisionist thinking online, much of it expressed with great humanity, I have read nothing that has made me question my conviction that Germany started the war in Europe because this was what Hitler and the Nazis wanted to do. They were not forced to go to war; they had ideological motives for doing so. The Allied bombing campaign was a brutal but necessary response to that aggression, designed to end the misery of the continent in the shortest possible period of time by destroying the capacity of the German nation to resist. No other viable strategy was available, given the technology and resources of the day and Germany is lucky not to have been subjected to attacks with atomic bombs.

It is also worth noting that Allied bombing capabilities were developed largely in response to Germany's own aerial bombing arm, which had demonstrated its potential in Spain during the civil war there, a development symbolized by the devastating bombing of Guernica on 26 April 1937, leading to widespread civilian deaths and injuries. Shocked by this tactic, Allied planners drew many important lessons from these events and later from the deliberate bombing of Rotterdam by the Luftwaffe in May 1940 and subsequently from the effects of the German Blitz on British cities that commenced in September 1940. The British response to these developments was primarily defensive at first, focusing on radar and improved fighter defences, and large-scale strategic bombing did not get underway in a serious way until two years after the Blitz; Bomber Command was simply not ready.

Despite Germany's earlier use of bombing civilian areas as a tactic, both Hitler and the Luftwaffe commander, Hermann Göring, were wary of the RAF and at the commencement of the aerial campaign against Britain both men issued very clear instructions to their forces regarding the tactics to be used, which included avoiding unnecessary civilian casualties. Soon, heavy losses forced the Luftwaffe to increase the use of night bombing, and with this change, accuracy and navigation were seriously impeded. Thus, on the fateful night of 24 August 1940, a small group of German bombers sent to target oil depots in the east of London, a legitimate military target, went astray and accidentally dropped their bombs on civilian homes in the East End of the city. The following night, on Churchill's orders, Bomber Command flew a retaliatory raid and bombed Berlin, the first of a series of small-scale night raids on Germany.

Hitler was incensed by the RAF attacks. At the height of his powers, with most of Western Europe under his control, this was a loss of face he simply would not tolerate. In a speech delivered in Berlin on 4 September 1940, Hitler explained what his response would be. Starting slowly and deliberately, as was his style, he first listed his and Germany's military achievements to that date. He then explained Britain's survival as being attributable only to an accident of geography – the defensive barrier provided by the English

Channel – and the speed of their retreat from France. The British were, in other words, cowering from German might behind that barrier and it was this fact that denied the Wehrmacht an opportunity to meet the British Army in open combat.

Hitler then explained that he had not responded to the British bombing attacks initially because, 'I was of the opinion that they would ultimately stop this nonsense'. He went on to explain that his patience was now at an end and that he had ordered that British 'night piracy' be countered by a full-scale night bombing offensive against the British mainland, saying, 'But this is a game at which two can play. When the British Air Force drops 2,000, or 3,000, or 4,000 kg of bombs, then we will drop 150,000, 180,000, 230,000, 300,000, 400,000 kg on a single night! When they declare they will attack our cities in great measure, we will eradicate their cities. The hour will come when one of us will break – and it will not be National Socialist Germany!' The crowd roared its approval. With this escalation, the die was cast, and each side would now do its best to force the other to capitulate, using the only effective weapons to hand in the circumstances; aircraft, submarines and ships.

Whether the Allied strategic bombing campaign shortened the war, or merely increased the suffering of the German civilian population, could only be assessed after the war had ended and it is a topic that will be debated by historians for the rest of time. I find it difficult to imagine that the destruction and havoc wrought by the bombing campaign did not have a huge effect on Nazi Germany's ability to give battle, almost certainly making the difference between an Allied victory and a bloody stalemate. I suggest that it was the lesser of two evils by a very large margin and if Germans wish to attribute blame for its effects to anyone, they need to pin that blame on one misguided group of people – Adolf Hitler and all who followed or tolerated him.

The Fires That Burned
Mark Johnson, 2013

All the fires burning
Co-mingling into one
The screaming of the children
Drowns out the bombers' hum

And even in the shelters
Flames eat the very air
From people into rag dolls;
Sans clothes, sans skin, sans hair

Yet who are we to judge those
Who bomb them from above?
They merely do their duty
To save the ones they love.

Chapter 7

Lost Over Europe

'I do not want to become guilty of blasphemy, but I ask: Who is greater, Christ or Hitler? By His death Christ had twelve disciples, who even (then) did not stay faithful. But Hitler today has a people of 70 million behind him. We cannot tolerate that another organization, which has another spirit than ours, should come into existence. National Socialism seriously lays this claim: I am the Lord, your God, you shall have no other Gods beside me ... Ours is the Kingdom, because we have a strong army, and the glory, because we are a respected people again, and this is as God wants it, in eternity. Heil Hitler!'

SS Obersturmbannführer Karl Schulz, a highly placed SS orator, during a lecture titled '*Ours is the Kingdom and the Power and the Glory.*' Schulz was a member of the Nazi Reichstag during the war and until 1944 he was Einsatzleiter (Control Officer) in the Jewish ghetto Litzmannstadt (Lodz), in German occupied Poland.

He was alive. Blown out of his exploding Lancaster bomber unharmed, having been shot down by a German night fighter aircraft on the return from his bombing mission to Germany, Cy Grant saw the ground reaching up to gather him in. He instinctively grasped the release knob on his harness, turned it and slapped it hard, as he had been taught to do. The next thing he knew, he was running on firm ground with ghostly billowing folds of silk collapsing all around him. He had made a good landing in a cornfield south of Nieuw-Venneg, Holland.

Grant wriggled out of his parachute harness and hid in the cornfield for most of the day. He was aware that the Germans were searching for survivors of the crash and could hear them calling to each other as they beat through the fields and woods. His heart was pounding noisily in his chest and it seemed loud enough to give him away. His breathing was laboured. Grant had no idea what fate might await a black 'terror flier' at the hands of the German army, but he imagined that it might not be a pleasant one.

Like all of his comrades, Grant had been told to try and escape towards the south and to aim for neutral Spain, but this now seemed an impossible task. How was he expected to complete such a journey without attracting attention? In his current circumstances, starting out from Holland, he would have to cross the whole of occupied Belgium and France. Just escaping from the field he was hiding in at the moment seemed a difficult enough prospect.

Grant quickly realized that his only hope was to seek help from the Dutch population. Since he had never expected to be shot down, this wasn't something he had planned either, so he would have to improvise. In the early evening he managed to attract the attention of a passing Dutch farmer who beckoned him to jump the ditch separating them. The quick thinking farmer then thrust a spade into Grant's hand so it would appear from a distance that he was a farm hand. He then took Grant to his farm, where the Dutchman's wife tended a small cut on Grant's head and gave him his first meal since he had taken off the evening before.

Although Grant did not yet know it, the local Dutch police had already been informed of his presence on the farm and it was they who subsequently handed Grant over to the Germans, conveying him to the German military post on the back of their motorcycle. The German soldiers were surprisingly benign and he was not subjected to the harsh treatment he had feared. Grant was then taken to an interrogation centre in Amsterdam and held in solitary confinement for five days, at one point being dragged out into bright sunshine to be photographed. This photo was later published in a German newspaper over the caption, 'A member of the Royal Air Force of indeterminate race' and this phrase would become the title for Grant's memoirs of his time in the RAF. A few days later he was transported, along with many other prisoners of war, to the Stalag Luft III prison camp, which was later the scene of *The Great Escape*. He was intimidated but unharmed.

Grant was not the only West Indian or West African volunteer to enter the German prisoner of war system. The tale of Johnny Smythe is recounted later, but other PoWs included Randolph Abbot of Trinidad, who died in his camp in November 1943 and Basil Anderson, also from that island, shot down and taken prisoner on 8 October 1943. G. A. Barrow of Barbados was captured on 17 September 1942 and Edgill Carrington of Trinidad, on 26 July 1943. A number of others who had joined from the Caribbean are also recorded as having become PoWs, but several of these appear to have been British men living or working in the region when the war broke out. Making this distinction has been one of the challenges faced in producing this work and so, when a man is not clearly listed as originating from the Caribbean, or shown in a photograph, I have tended to err on the side of caution and not describe him as a Caribbean volunteer.

Pilot Officer Mike Guilfoyle of 12 Squadron, whom RAF records list as originating from 4 Winchester Road, Half Way Tree, Kingston, Jamaica, was a 'white Jamaican' who had volunteered from the Jamaican civil service in the early 1940s. Now aged twenty-three, Guilfoyle was the pilot of Lancaster ND242, which crashed near Paris on the night of 27/28 June 1944, three and a half weeks after the Allied D-Day landings had taken place in Normandy. The aircraft had developed engine trouble about half an hour from the target. Flying at 12,000 feet, the cockpit crew noticed that the oil pressure in one engine was falling and they 'feathered' the engine, turning it off. The propeller stopped spinning and they were now flying on three engines, losing height slowly.

Guilfoyle continued to guide the plane towards the target, the Paris/Vaires railway yard at Vaires–sur–Marne, on the eastern outskirts of Paris. It was a dark night, the full moon still being almost two weeks away, but as they flew over the railway yards the crew could just make out the railway tracks glinting in a steel web below them, illuminated by flares. Moments before they dropped their bombs, a second engine began to spew white and yellow flames. The bombs fell away and the pilot feathered this second propeller as he turned the aircraft back towards home.

Almost immediately, a third engine displayed a coolant leak and it too had to be feathered. They were now flying the heavy bomber on a single engine and although they had not sensed the impact, it seemed certain that enemy fire must account for at least two of the engines going out of action. Within two minutes they had descended to 7,000 feet and their rate of descent was accelerating. It was clear that they could never make it home in this state and that their plane was about to hit to ground.

The order to abandon the aircraft was given and while Guilfoyle held the aircraft steady, assisted by the flight engineer, the other five crewmen jumped safely from the front hatch and from the entrance door. Now came the critical moment for the remaining flight crew, as they needed to leave the aircraft to fly itself while they clambered out. The ground was even closer than before and they could see trees, fields, roads, streams and houses all rushing by a few thousand feet below them. There wasn't a second to spare.

The flight engineer restarted one of the damaged engines in order to keep the plane level for a few moments longer while he and the pilot jumped. The engineer left first and once his parachute had opened he looked about him and saw the pilot suspended from his own parachute a short distance away. All seven of the crew landed unhurt. Guilfoyle, his navigator Joe Sonshine, and their rear gunner Dougie Jordin, were all taken prisoner after being betrayed to the Germans by Frenchmen. All three men were eventually taken to Buchenwald concentration camp, known for its brutality and gruesome medical experiments on prisoners. Here, Guilfoyle was held along with 167 other Allied prisoners from Great Britain, the United States, Australia, Canada and New Zealand. Classified by the SS as 'terror fliers' and spies, the airmen were judged to be criminals. They were not accorded PoW status and a sentence of death was rumoured to have been passed on them. After six weeks living in deplorable conditions, the senior RAF officer in the group, Squadron Leader Lamasson, a New Zealander, was able to get word of their predicament to the nearest Luftwaffe base. Lamasson had also been shot down during a raid on a Parisian rail marshalling yard on 8 June 1944 and he had attempted to evade capture by making for Spain. However, he was double-crossed by a member of the French Résistance and handed over to the Germans in exchange for a payment of 10,000 Francs.

Two Luftwaffe officers visited Buchenwald in response to Lamasson's report, on the pretence that they were inspecting bomb damage, and they spoke directly to Lamasson. Convinced that the Allied prisoners were genuine aircrew and not spies, these officers reported their findings to Berlin and an outraged Herman Göring demanded that the aircrew prisoners be immediately transferred to the Luftwaffe's Stalag Luft III camp, where they were held as conventional PoWs. This was not before two of the RAF men

Arthur Young. Born in Cardiff, he was killed in the crash of the 'Salford Lancaster' on 30 July 1944, while returning to base from a raid on German positions in Normandy.

Vincent Bunting chatting with the South African Ace, 'Sailor' Malan. Born in Panama and raised in Jamaica, Bunting flew Spitfires with 132 Sqn. He survived the war. Malan later became active in the anti-apartheid movement. (Courtesy of WASP)

Billy Strachan (left of picture) of Kingston Jamaica and also 99 and 156 Sqns with his crew. A bomber pilot with 45 missions over Europe, Strachan survived the war. (Courtesy of Mrs Audrey Dewjee)

Accurate bombing could be achieved when the conditions were right and the crews well trained. Here, a port is struck by 9 Sqn aircraft. (Courtesy of IX Squadron, RAF)

Even in daylight, bombing accurately through smoke or cloud was extremely difficult. (Courtesy of IX Squadron, RAF)

The results of bombing on the centre of the German city of Cologne, February 1945.

Eugene Bullard, the first black American flier, who served with the French during the First World War.

Flt Lt John Blair DFC of Jamaica and formerly of No 102 Sqn RAF Bomber Command, attending the VJ Day Parade in London, 1995. (Author)

Blair family members visit the seaside, St Elizabeth, Jamaica, 1930s. (Author)

Flt Sgt Lincoln Lynch of Jamaica served as an Air Gunner with 102 Sqn RAF Bomber Command between 1944 and 1945. He shot down a German night fighter on his first operational mission and was awarded the DFM for his courage under fire. (Courtesy of WASP)

The Giessen rail yards in Germany, shown in March 1945, following an attack in which John Blair's No 102 Sqn participated.

John Blair (left of photo) during his training in Canada 1942. The aircraft behind appears to be an Anson which was used for flight and navigator training. (Author)

A typical Jamaican female school girl's Hockey Team in 1945 close to the spot where Canadian soldier Tom Forsyth was warned off watching girl's hockey practice. John Blair's niece, Barbara Johnson, is 2nd from left in this photo. (Author)

John Blair & crew with their Comet aircraft, 1960s. (Author)

John Blair briefs
for a Transport
Command flight,
early 1960s.
(Author)

John Blair in training, Canada, 1942. (Author)

Lyndon Pounder of Trinidad and 149 Sqn (navigator) helped to drop food supplies to the starving Dutch population during 'Operation Manna' in May 1945. (Courtesy of David Pounder)

A crew from No 2 Sqn RAF undergoes a typical post-mission intelligence debriefing, 1940s. (Courtesy of II Sqn RAF)

Carl Chantrielle from Jamaica served as a code operator with RAF signals after training at Filey in Yorkshire. He later became the President of Cable & Wireless, Jamaica. (Courtesy of Carl Chantrielle)

Typical RAF squadron bosses, 1940s. (Courtesy of II Sqn RAF)

A group of Caribbean aircrew volunteers. Ulric Cross, DSO, DFM, of 139 Sqn is seated third from right in the front row. (Courtesy of Mrs Audrey Dewjee)

The Teacher's Cottage in rural Jamaica that John Blair once lived in as a child. (Author)

A typical Jamaican schoolboy (in this case, the author's father), mid-1940s. (Author)

A typical Jamaican schoolgirl, mid 1940s. (Author)

The role model. A No 2 Sqn Spitfire pilot, 1940s (Courtesy of II Sqn RAF)

The cockpit of an RAF training aircraft, 1930s. (Courtesy of II Sqn RAF)

Caribbean aircrew trainees, Canada, 1942. John Blair is standing, 2nd from left in the middle row, while Orville Lynch is at the extreme right of the same row. (Author)

Norma and Arthur Wint at their wedding in England, 1945. Flight Lt. Wint, from Jamaica, was an RAF pilot during the war who went on to win gold at the 1948 Olympics. (Author)

Flt Lt John J Blair, DFC completed his full tour and remained with the RAF until the 1960s. (Author)

Group Captain Larry Osbourne of Coastal Command became the most senior of the West Indian volunteers. (Courtesy of WASP)

Flight Sergeants Weeks (left) of Barbados and Joseph (right) of Trinidad pictured with a Spitfire. Weeks survived the war but Joseph was killed over Holland in May 1944. (Courtesy of WASP)

Basil Johnson of the Bahamas applied three times to the RAF before successfully gaining entry as a flight engineer. (Courtesy of the Johnson family)

had died at Buchenwald, where the airmen had had their heads shaved and then been starved and forced to sleep in the open for three weeks.

The other four crewmen from Guilfoyle's Lancaster all evaded capture and made their way back to British soil. The flight engineer, who had landed so close to Guilfoyle, got away from the Germans in the dark and was the first to arrive back in Britain. He was followed by the bomb aimer, wireless operator and mid-upper gunner. That gunner, Leslie Faircloth of Croydon in south London, had been taken in by Frenchmen and provided with food, false papers and railway tickets. He eventually met members of the French Résistance who also helped him on his way towards neutral Spain, although at another stage in his trek a Frenchman identified him as being English and reported him to the German Army. It seems that such actions were commonplace. Faircloth escaped the cottage he was staying in by the back door as German soldiers entered through the front. He hid in the woods and watched the Germans searching for him all night. Finally, on 13 July 1944, after two weeks on the run, Faircloth crossed the Spanish border and gave himself up to border guards. After a further week in Spanish custody, a British Vice Consul rescued him and Faircloth was sent home by way of Gibraltar, arriving in Britain on 10 August after an epic journey. Guilfoyle himself was not released by advancing British troops until May 1945. (From interviews with Les Faircloth by his son, Paul Faircloth.)

Most of the Allied aircrews had been shot down by a highly skilled, seasoned Luftwaffe enemy, who was deployed in aerial defence of the Reich along what was known as the Kammhuber Line, supported by thousands of anti-aircraft guns and searchlights on the ground. The Kammhuber Line was a series of boxes on the map, each approximately twenty miles wide, stretching from Denmark in the north, to the Bay of Biscay in the south. Each box contained three radar units; a Freya unit for long-range detection of groups of incoming planes, and two short-range Würzburg units, one for tracking selected RAF raiders and the other for tracking the Luftwaffe night fighters. Using the signals data from these devices, the German ground-based flight controllers could calculate the flight paths and travel times of all aircraft detected and direct the night fighters towards intercept points. Even when directed right onto an enemy raid, however, the German pilots still faced the difficult task of actually spotting enemy aircraft in the dark skies of

Europe. When RAF losses were high, the path of the raid was often marked by a trail of burning aircraft on the ground, a string of funeral pyres, perhaps thirty or forty in all, stretching from Germany to the coast of Holland and clearly visible from 20,000 feet. Somewhere along that line of fires flew the British heavy bombers.

In amongst an invisible stream of up to one thousand bombers, the Luftwaffe Nachtjager crews would snoop, eyes peeled for any glimmer or light, or for the shape of a bomber against the sky or ground. Then they would close in and if they were not chased off by alert and accurate RAF gunners, their cannon and rocket fire would tear into the thin skin of the airborne target, smashing airframe, wiring, equipment and men indiscriminately, either setting it on fire, bringing it down or causing it to explode in mid-air.

By 1943, Johnny Smythe of Sierra Leone had been promoted to Flying Officer, but during his twenty-eighth bombing mission with 623 Squadron over Berlin, on the night of 18 November, his luck also ran out when enemy night fighters patrolling their section of the Kammhuber Line intercepted his bomber:

'We were flying at 16,000 ft when the fighters came out of nowhere. They raked the fuselage and there were flames everywhere. Then the searchlights caught us. I was hit by shrapnel. Pieces came from underneath, piercing my abdomen, going through my side. Another came through my seat and into my groin. I heard the pilot ordering us to bail out. We'd had some rough ones before but this seemed to be the end.'

Smythe was able to drag himself to the hatch and escape the doomed aircraft, parachuting safely to the ground, where he then hid in a nearby barn. But his arrival had been observed:

'Men in (German) uniform came into the barn where I was hiding behind some straw. The Germans couldn't believe their eyes. I'm sure that's what saved me from being shot immediately. To see a black man in uniform – and an officer at that – was more than they could come to terms with. They just stood there gazing at me.'

Less fortunate than either Grant or Smythe was Grey Doyle Cumberbatch, a black Barbadian volunteer and the son of Charles Wilkinson and Octavia C. Cumberbatch, of St. Michael, Barbados. Cumberbatch was a sergeant, serving as an air bomber (bomb aimer) with No. 100 Squadron, which operated Lancaster bombers and his aircraft, Lancaster ED549, was the first squadron Lancaster to be lost during the war. The plane went down on its return from a mine laying mission to St. Nazaire on 5 March 1943 while apparently trying to land at Langar Airfield, Nottinghamshire, although it was not on the correct approach. It was one of two aircraft lost by 100 Squadron on that operation. The crash was witnessed by an air raid warden named Dennis Kirk, who rushed to the scene after an aircraft that sounded as though it was in trouble flew low overhead and then crashed into the ground about a quarter of a mile distant. When he arrived at the crash site, Kirk found one dazed survivor sitting on the railway line who told him that they had dropped their bombs on the target and there were therefore no explosives left on board. All the other crewmen lay dead inside the wreckage, with Cumberbatch among them. Pieces of German cannon shell were later found in the wreck, indicating that the plane was probably attacked and damaged by an enemy night fighter. Sergeant Cumberbatch was 21-years-old at the time of his death. He is buried in Long Bennington, St. Swithin Churchyard, in Lincolnshire, along with two Canadian members of his crew, Flight Sergeants Gerald Russell Avery and Rene Rodger Landry, both of Ontario.

No. 9 Squadron Bomber Command was home to at least four Caribbean volunteer aircrew during 1943, all of whom died on operations that year. The squadron would claim its most famous prize in November 1944, when it helped to sink the mighty and greatly feared German ship *Tirpitz*, the second of two Bismarck–class battleships built for the German Kriegsmarine and considered a major threat to Allied shipping. No less than ten separate operations were mounted against the ship, including midget submarine attacks, carrier-based attacks and conventional air raids by heavy bombers, but the expertise that 9 Squadron would demonstrate – when, along with aircraft from other RAF squadrons, it dropped 12,000 'Tallboy' bombs onto and beside the German vessel in a Norwegian fjord, causing it to capsize as a result of flooding – was developed and honed during the great air battles of 1942 and 1943.

There can be few better examples of the kind of heroism displayed by the men of Bomber Command than that provided by Flight Sergeant George Thompson, who was a 9 Squadron wireless operator during a raid on the Dortmund-Ems Canal on 1 January 1945, in which John Blair and 102 Squadron would also take part. Although Thompson had no connection with the Caribbean, his citation for bravery provides an extraordinary insight into the dangers all fliers shared and the demands that might be made of any of them at any moment.

The citation records that the bombs had only just been released when a heavy flak shell hit the aircraft just in front of the mid-upper turret. This was effectively dead centre of the aircraft and very close to the recently emptied bomb bay, between the wireless operator, navigator, pilot, engineer and bomb aimer in the forward section and the air gunners in the middle and rear. Fire and smoke filled the fuselage, blinding most of the crew, but at that moment another shell hit the Lancaster, this time in the nose. There was a sudden and powerful inrush of freezing air, the temperature at 20,000 feet typically being in the region of -15° Celsius. The screaming wind cleared the smoke away and a scene of utter devastation was revealed. Most of the perspex screen of the nose compartment had been blown away and there were gaping holes in the roof of the cockpit above the pilot's head. The pilot, however, was unharmed, but because the intercom wiring was shredded, no communication with the air gunners was possible. If that was not enough, there were fires within the aircraft, machine-gun rounds were cooking off in the heat and exploding and one engine was also alight. There was also a large hole in the floor of the aircraft. In short, they were lucky to still be in level flight.

Thompson peered down the length of the aircraft's interior and made out the shape of the mid-upper gunner slumped in his turret, seemingly unconscious and on fire. Rather than focusing on quelling the fire and thus seeing to his own safety, he raced down the fuselage, using his bare hands to hold onto the metal frame of the aircraft as he made his way around the hole in the floor, and then heading directly into the flames and exploding ammunition surrounding the gunner. He pulled the gunner from the blazing turret and dragged him away from the flames. Then, with his bare hands unprotected by gloves or anything else, he beat out the flames on the gunner's burning clothing, sustaining serious burns to his face, hands and legs in the process. He had now become a casualty himself.

With the mid-upper gunner now relatively safe, Thompson looked further down the aircraft towards the tail. He could see that the rear turret was also on fire and despite his own painful injuries, he forced himself to move to the rear of the aircraft where he found the tail gunner unconscious and alight. Once again, Thompson used his bare hands, already badly burned, to beat out the fire on a comrade's clothing.

Although exhausted and in severe pain, Thompson decided that he must now return to the cockpit to report the situation to the captain of the aircraft. He went back through the burning fuselage and navigated his way around the hole in the floor a second time. Now, his hands were causing him excruciating pain and his progress was almost certainly slower than before. Perhaps as a consequence frostbite developed and his condition when he finally made the cockpit was later described as being so pitiful that even his captain failed to recognize him. He made his report and was then given the limited medical attention possible until the aircraft landed.

Flight Sergeant Thompson died of his injuries three weeks later. One of the gunners also died, but the other was saved and he owed his life to Thompson, who was posthumously awarded the Victoria Cross for his gallantry.

The first recorded Caribbean aircrew loss from 9 Squadron was that of Sergeant George Nunez, the pilot of Lancaster ED838 and this was also the first 9 Squadron aircraft to go missing following their move to the newly opened airfield at Bardney. (Nunez is listed in the 9 Squadron Operations Record Book as a Sergeant, although other sources record his rank as Pilot Officer. It is likely that his promotion was in the pipeline at the time of his death.) Bardney would be the squadron's home between 14 April 1943 and 6 July 1945. A Trinidadian volunteer, George Nunez appears in photographs to have been of mixed race and his surname suggests a possible South American connection, Trinidad lying just off the coast of Venezuela. He was the child of Albert and Georgiana Nunez and was married to Olive Adella Nunez, also of Trinidad.

Just after midnight on 1 May 1943, aircraft from 9 Squadron, including Lancaster ED838 with Nunez at the controls, took off to join a raid on the key city of Essen, home of the giant Krupp armaments factory in the heart of the Ruhr. This mission, which involved 305 aircraft, formed part of the Battle of the Ruhr, a five month campaign against Germany's industrial heartland and an area housing a multitude of coke plants, steelworks, synthetic oil plants and heavy industrial complexes. The destruction of these cities, as well as the civilian communities that surrounded them and housed their workforces, was deemed a strategic priority for the Allies. The bombing had to be carried out through cloud, based on the position of flares dropped by Pathfinder aircraft, a common procedure, but the glow of fires through the cloud and the good concentration of explosions suggested a successful attack to those taking part.

There was heavy flak over Essen during this raid and several aircraft returned to base with holes in the wings and fuselage. Nunez and his crew were lost without trace and all seven are commemorated on the Air Forces Memorial at Runnymede, which overlooks the River Thames in Surrey, along with another 20,000 airmen lost over Europe who have no known graves. Essen itself was devastated by a long series of such raids, its factories reduced to piles of rubble and twisted steel and its surviving civilian workers traumatized, bereaved and in desperate need of housing, medicines and foodstuffs. Many years would pass before the city recovered from the terrible effects of Allied bombing.

Not two months after the death of George Nunez, Caribbean volunteer Sergeant Charles P. King from Barbados, a West Indian of European descent, joined the long list of fatal casualties when his 9 Squadron aircraft, Lancaster ED831, went down on the night of 25 June 1943 while attacking Gelsenkirchen, a centre of coal production and oil refining close to Essen, which was frequently visited by Bomber Command. It was during this same raid that Cy Grant was shot down and taken prisoner. All eight men on board King's Lancaster, including Squadron Leader A. M. Hobbs, were killed when the aircraft was downed by Luftwaffe Hauptman August Geiger, near Ijsselmeer, twenty kilometers east-south-east of Edam, Holland.

The 9 Squadron aircraft had taken off from Bardney at 2230 hours to join another 472 aircraft taking part. One member of the crew, a Sergeant Sams, had reported to the squadron that very afternoon from an operational training unit and this was his first flight with them. As the bomber stream made its way towards that night's target, Luftwaffe Ace Geiger was already airborne, patrolling a box through which he hoped the raid would pass. After spending some time flying in the dark in silence, maintaining a quiet cockpit, Geiger heard the voice of his ground controller through his headphones. Information about the course, current location, altitude, and probable target was conveyed to all night fighter pilots in the vicinity. Geiger turned to intercept, a shark after a shoal of fish, and with his eyes peeled he began to search the black skies for anything that might reveal the location of an enemy. Suddenly, a large black shape materialized ahead and he altered course, speed and altitude to bring his fighter in below and behind the British four engine bomber. Then, with a short squeeze on the trigger, he sent a stream of cannon shells into the belly of the enemy plane and watched as it burst into flame, dipped to port and fell to earth in a rapidly accelerating spin. There was no chance of anyone surviving the dive and the German pilot would be able to chalk up yet another victory on landing, but his mind was already on the next target and he wheeled through the sky seeking fresh prey. Geiger, who would eventually claim forty-nine such aircraft kills, was himself shot down and killed later the same year, in September 1943.

Leslie F. Gilkes was the son of Joseph and Octavia Gilkes, of Siparia, Trinidad and he had volunteered for service in 1942, before being trained in Trinidad at the RAF air station at Piarco. Now flying with 9 Squadron as an air gunner in a Lancaster piloted by a Scottish sergeant named David McKenzie, Gilkes and his crew were on their seventh mission, heading to Hamburg on the night of 2 August 1943, when they encountered violent electrical storms and heavy cloud. They also had to contend with severe icing. The attackers were unable to locate the target with certainty, but they bombed through the clouds and they were able to make out the glow of fires below. It seemed that something flammable had been hit, but the raid was later judged unsuccessful by RAF intelligence officers.

Flying back to its base and well to the south of the assigned route for the bomber stream, Gilkes' aircraft was intercepted in the dark of the night by Luftwaffe Ace and holder of the Knight's Cross, Oberfeldwebel Karl-Heinz Scherfling, a man who would go on to claim a total of thirty-three victories over Allied aircraft before being killed in July 1944. Scherfling manoeuvred his Messerschmitt 110 night fighter aircraft into an attack position, most probably behind and below the bomber and in its blind spot. He then fired his upward mounted cannons. The RAF aircraft plunged twenty thousand feet into the sea just off the Dutch coast, near the island of Texel. All seven men on board were killed and at least four of them are said to have been buried in Holland. Gilkes body was never recovered, but he is remembered on the Runnymede Memorial.

Pilot Officer Allan Duncan of Jamaica and all six of his 9 Squadron crewmates, flying in Lancaster DV332, piloted by Flight Lieutenant R. Wells, probably met a similar fate on the night of 2 December 1943 when their bomber went missing on a major raid to Berlin. Duncan, who was twenty-five years of age when he died, hailed from the district of Above Rocks, not far from the capital city of Kingston and nestled in the lush green hilly country that makes up most of the island. The son of Eustace and Ellen Duncan, Allan had successfully qualified as a navigator and this was his assigned role within his crew. Nothing was heard from DV332 after take-off, but the crew were buried in the Berlin 1939–1945 War Cemetery, so it is evident that they arrived near or over the target before being shot down.

This attack, in which a total of twelve aircraft from 9 Squadron participated, successfully bombed the German capital from a height of 21,000 feet, dropping the explosives in spite of cloud obscuring the green and red target indicators placed by the Pathfinder Force. Surviving 9 Squadron crews reported that the Pathfinder's markers had been well concentrated, as was the bombing, with several large fires being ignited in the city. In fact, strong crosswinds had caused most of the Pathfinder markers to drift and miss the target, falling to the south of Berlin, although two Siemens factories, a ball-bearing plant and railway installations were damaged by the raid. The main force bomber crews had in all likelihood dropped their loads accurately on the target indicators, but the markers themselves were in the wrong place.

This major raid on Berlin was one of a series of sixteen massed attacks directed at the city by Bomber Command between November 1943 and March 1944, in what became known as the 'Battle of Berlin'. Describing it as a knockout blow that would trigger a German surrender, Bomber Command's commander, Arthur Harris, predicted that, 'It will cost us between 400 and 500 aircraft. It will cost Germany the war.' In fact, the RAF lost more than 500 bombers during these operations, along with 2,690 aircrew killed and an estimated 1,000 captured. Bomber Command's losses during the battle exceeded the five per cent threshold considered sustainable and the losses suffered over Berlin during this five month period accounted for seven per cent of all Bomber Command losses between 1939 and 1945.

The RAF's attacks on Berlin caused immense loss of life and widespread devastation in the city and even today it has not recovered its pre-war appearance. Just ten days prior to Allan Duncan's death, the second major raid of the battle had killed at least 2,000 Berliners and left more than 175,000 people homeless, mainly in areas to the west of the city centre, including Tiergarten and Charlottenburg, Schöneberg and Spandau. A further 1,000 people were killed and another 100,000 made homeless by the third raid, which took place the very next night, but important industrial and administrative buildings were also destroyed, as were storage depots. Estimates for the total number of Berliners killed during the course of the battle vary widely, but even the most conservative figures put the losses at 4,000 killed, 10,000 injured, and almost half a million made homeless, while other sources claim that the numbers were almost twice that high. Because of the RAF loss rate the Battle of Berlin is normally cited as a German victory, but with the harm inflicted to Germany's own population and critical infrastructure, this victory was at best pyrrhic.

While the details of what befell Allan Duncan's crew are not known, another crew from 9 Squadron, flying out of RAF Bardney in Lincolnshire, reported a sharp encounter with a German night fighter on their way to Berlin that night. Lancaster 'Y' was captained by Pilot Officer Bayldon and at 2013 hours the pilot picked up a warning signal on his 'special apparatus' (presumably radar) telling him that an unknown aircraft was closing from behind. He warned the gunners over the intercom and immediately started evasive manoeuvres, corkscrewing the heavily laden aircraft through the sky in order to put off the attacker's aim. Unlike today, Bomber Command aircraft under threat from enemy fighters did not jettison their loads in order to evade more effectively – they pushed on towards the target, bombs and all, bombs on target being judged more valuable than live flyers returning to base, within certain margins.

A few seconds after the initial warning from Bayldon, both the mid-upper and the tail gunner spotted a German night fighter closing on them at a range of about 800 yards. The German pilot opened fire with cannon and machine guns, the tracer rounds passing just over the bomber. The German also fired a rocket shell at the RAF plane, but this burnt out short of the Lancaster and fell away. Both RAF gunners now returned fire, firing several bursts of machine gun ammunition at the night fighter, which turned left and climbed away into the darkness to seek other prey. It was not spotted again by Bayldon or his crew and neither aircraft was damaged during the duel. Nevertheless, of the 425 Lancasters involved in this particular raid, thirty-seven were lost, a toll of 8.7 per cent, and it is entirely possible that Allan Duncan's aircraft fell victim to the night fighter that attacked Bayldon, as all three aircraft were operating in the same part of the sky at the same time.

Another 9 Squadron aircraft, DV334, piloted by Pilot Officer Warwick, joined the list of casualties for the 2 December raid when it crashed in fog, twenty-five miles off course and out of fuel, on its return to England, again with the loss of all eight crew. Six of these men died in the crash, while the two survivors died of their injuries shortly after. The aircraft was attempting to land at RAF Gamston in Nottinghamshire when it hit the ground. One of the crew members, Sergeant D. Munn (nicknamed 'Chumley'), had spent part of the previous night insistently telling a friend on ground crew, presumably female, that he was convinced he would be killed on his next operation. Exactly what combination of fog, flak, fighters, fuel, icing, error, systems or mechanical failure conspired to bring down this aircraft will never be known and nor will the difficult choices the crew might have had to make in the minutes before they perished.

Of course, other RAF squadrons suffered equal or even heavier losses than 9 Squadron and many of them also counted Caribbean and West African volunteers amongst their crews. On 22 October 1943, Pilot Officer Bruce Fitzgerald Henry Miller, DFC, another black Barbadian volunteer serving with No. 103 Squadron, flew from Elsham Wolds on a night bombing operation over Germany. The raid started when 569 RAF aircraft took off from the south of England, heading for Kassel. Over the target area the RAF aircraft dropped 350 aerial mines whose descent was retarded by the use of a parachute so that they would explode at ground level, 600 high explosive bombs and 417,000 incendiary devices. Within fifteen minutes the entire Kassel city centre was a sea of fire and an estimated 10,000 residents lost their lives in an attack that lasted a mere fifty-four minutes.

German fighters then vigorously attacked the raiders above Wesertal on their homeward leg and pursued the bombers doggedly through the night sky. Witnesses on the ground would have heard the rattle of cannon fire above them. Miller's Lancaster was attacked by one of these night fighters and his aircraft exploded in mid-air after receiving numerous hits. It crashed in the district of Rischenau and all seven RAF crew members died. They were reburied after the war in the British Military Cemetery in Hanover. Bruce Miller was married to Helen Elizabeth Miller of Sawley, Long Eaton, in Derbyshire.

Not all of those RAF aircrew killed on such operations fell victim to enemy fire. Merely flying and attacking ground targets could be fatal, even without any intervention by the other side. Taking off at 0215 hours on 8 August 1944, nine Mosquito aircraft of No. 107 Squadron flew to attack the railway sidings near Montmiral, Marne, in occupied France. Aboard Mosquito NS280 were the pilot, Flying Officer Wilburn Taylor from Saskatoon, Saskatchewan and the navigator, Karl Aiken, of Kingston, Jamaica. Karl was the son of Eugene and Louise Aiken and after joining up in December 1941 he had been commissioned in the RAF on 28 August 1943, less than a year before this flight.

The attack was successful and the planes put a long section of French railway line out of action, hitting five trains in the process and starting a fire one mile in length. However, Flying Officer Taylor was reportedly well known for his dare devil flying at low altitude and as his aircraft made its attack on the railway line, it seems to have hit a telephone pole and burst into flames. Another pilot reported seeing an aircraft hit the ground, off to one side of the attack, burning as it went in. Both crewmen probably died instantly and they are buried at Connantre Communal Cemetery, France. Aiken was 24-years-old and Taylor was 29-years-old.

Born in Cardiff in 1923, black British airman Arthur Young had joined the RAF in 1941 aged eighteen. He began signals training in Morse code, with a posting in Blackpool. His wireless training began in July 1942 and by 1943 he was a qualified wireless operator/air gunner with Bomber Command. Arthur's family origins are unclear, but he was quite possibly descended from the black population that settled around many of the ports of England during the 250 years of the slave trade. He might also have been a child of immigrants from the colonies, but this is less likely because immigration at that time was far more restricted than it became after the war. In March 1944, Arthur Young had married Florence May Silver, also of Cardiff and by then he had been flying operationally for some time.

On Sunday, 30 July 1944, 692 RAF aircraft were sent to bomb German defensive positions prior to an American-led ground attack in the Villers Bocage – Caumont area of Normandy. The Allies had landed in France on 6 June, but stiff German resistance had so far kept them penned on the Normandy beachhead. Heavy bombing of the German front line was one of the keys to achieving a breakout into the French countryside.

Thick cloud hindered the attack and only 377 of the attacking aircraft were able to bomb their targets. Of these, only two out of six targets were effectively hit for the loss of four RAF Lancaster bombers. Shortly after 1000 hours that morning, Arthur Young's Lancaster bomber, PB304, part of No. 106 Squadron, was limping back to its base, having aborted its attack due to the cloud, before developing engine trouble somewhere over Manchester, England. Witnesses on the ground saw the plane descending and sensed that it was in trouble from the noise of its engines. The heavily laden four engine bomber crashed into Littleton Road Playing Fields on the banks of the River Irwell in Salford. Arthur Young, just 21-years-old, was killed along with the rest of his seven man crew when the aircraft, still carrying a 9,000lb bomb load and a great deal of fuel, exploded on impact. The explosion was heard several miles away.

The disaster shook the people of Salford as two local people were killed on the ground when the explosion destroyed their house and also because one of the crew members lived only two miles away from the scene. In addition to Young, the crew of the Lancaster included a volunteer reserve from Purley in Surrey, a coal miner's son from Pendlebury, a farmer from Shropshire and a medical student from the Punjab in India. Flight Lieutenant Peter Lines was the pilot and had only just begun to take part in operations, flying his first raid against caves housing German flying bombs at St Leu d'Esserant earlier in July, while his tail gunner, Sergeant Mohand Singh, the Punjabi, had been with the RAF since 1941 and had completed twenty-two of his mandated thirty operations before the Salford crash.

Also on board the doomed plane were the flight engineer, Sergeant Peter Barnes, who had served in both Iraq and Ceylon as ground crew; navigator, Flying Officer Harry Reid, a Canadian born to Scottish parents; and mid-upper-gunner, Sergeant John Bruce Thornley of Davenport, a former RAF cook who had volunteered for aircrew and completed his gunnery training in January 1944. The bomb aimer, Flying Officer John Harvey Steel was from Bradford, but he had learned his skills in America. A month before the crash, Steel had told his family of a premonition he had that he would not be coming home. A display at the Yorkshire Air Museum in Pocklington shows the photos of the crew and provides a few details about this crash and a memorial was erected at Agecroft Cemetery on Langley Road, Pendleton, in Salford. Joe Bamford, whose grandmother was one of the two civilians killed in the crash, has written a book titled *The Salford Lancaster*, detailing the events on that day and of the two weeks leading up to it.

Chapter 8

Black Prisoners of War

'I have been studying how I may compare
The prison where I live unto the world.'
William Shakespeare, King Richard II

Cy Grant arrived at the Stalag Luft III prisoner of war camp in July 1943. The camp was located in the middle of a pine forest near the town of Sagan, which is today in Poland. This large camp, exclusively used to house aircrew, was divided into six separate compounds, each containing fifteen barracks buildings. Three compounds were occupied by American flyers and the other three by RAF personnel:

'My arrival at the camp created a bit of a stir amongst the Germans. A black officer! The Commanding Officer sent for me. I was ushered into the presence of a very handsome middle-aged man, not the type of man one would have expected to see in charge of a prisoner of war camp. He had an intelligent, dignified manner and was extremely polite to me. He asked me where I came from and thrust a page of a German newspaper in front of me. It featured a picture of me, taken after five days of solitary confinement. Fame at last!

'There was no point now in not telling him where I came from. I told him I was from British Guyana. His face lit up. Unbelievably he had been there! I cannot remember what he had done there, but thereafter the Commanding Officer always saluted me whenever we chanced to meet on his rounds.'

The German officer was Oberst Friedrich Wilhelm Gustav von Lindeiner genannt von Wildau (or Colonel von Lindeiner for short). Once the German military governor for German East Africa, Grant was not the first black person he had encountered. The Colonel earned the respect of many of his prisoners for his professional conduct and when he was investigated after the war for possible involvement in war crimes, it was based on the testimony of former Allied PoWs that he was released.

Grant experienced no racism of any kind from either the German guards, his fellow prisoners, or his eventual Russian liberators, during his two years in captivity, with one exception; an American airman who was also being held in the camp insisted on calling him 'Nigger'. As Grant explained, this man was from the Deep South and he was never able to accommodate, in his own version of reality, the concept of a black officer who was a member of an operational flight crew.

Meanwhile, in Stalag Luft I, another prisoner-of-war camp for 9,000 men in Pomerania, Johnny Smythe helped on the escape committee, but could not break out himself:

'I don't think a six-foot-five black man would have got very far in Pomerania, somehow.'

Imperial War Museum Collection. 'Together' Collections, War in the Air Section, Personal Story 10, Johnny Smythe.

Several weeks after he arrived at Stalag Luft III, Grant was overjoyed to witness the arrival of his skipper, Al Langille. Although his neck had been broken, and his head was now permanently angled to one side, the charismatic Langille, a born leader of men, immediately took charge and picked his own group of prisoners to lodge and eat together, just as he had once selected his crew. The group comprised ten Canadians, an Irishman and Grant.

Langille was also very practical and the group soon had home-made cups, pots and pans and a working radio, built from scraps, with which they could now follow the course of the war. The prisoners received Red Cross parcels every week and the corned beef, tinned salmon, jams and cigarettes meant that they were much better supplied than their captors. Bribing of the guards was widespread and some German personnel actually enjoyed the company of their charges, often overstaying their welcome in the barracks. Many prisoners felt that it was actually they who were the privileged ones, with the

Germans effectively being supplicants to their charges, who were not only richer, but who obviously had a better future in store as the likely victors. The relationship between prisoner and captor continued to evolve as the war progressed and by the end of the war this reversal of roles was complete.

Apart from the twice daily parades, during which the men were counted, the officer prisoners were not required to work by the Germans and for most of the next two years they would be left to their own devices. The main activities included sports, classes on every subject under the sun, music and theatre, and tunnelling for escape. After six months, the men were moved to a nearby Offizierslager, or 'Oflag', a sub-camp specifically intended for officer ranks only. Those interred here were well educated and of above average intelligence, as well as being members of the RAF officer caste with military training and a culture of discipline to support them. Grant ran the music society for his block and his time in captivity was clearly a period of great personal growth.

Both the famous *Wooden Horse* escape and the much larger *Great Escape* took place from Stalag Luft III and a great deal of energy was expended by both sides, the one building real and diversionary tunnels and the other trying to detect them. It was the official duty of captured officers to attempt to escape but the aftermath of the *Great Escape* in 1944 permanently changed the mood in the camp. Relations between the prisoners and their German guards were irrevocably affected when fifty of the escapees were executed in cold blood by SS and Gestapo personnel after their recapture. Cy Grant:

'This news sent a wave of resentment and bitterness towards the Germans that never left us. Loud protestations were made by the Senior British Officer and a policy of non-cooperation came into effect. From henceforth we were as awkward as we could possibly be.
'On Thursday, 13 April, a memorial service was held immediately after the morning roll call on the sports ground. It took the form of a parade service. I cannot recall any parade, in captivity or out, which was executed with more solemnity and precision. Even thinking about it now is quite moving.'

The executed escapees were representative of the international makeup of the RAF at that time, although this is not always clearly communicated. Of the fifty men shot, no less than twenty-six were Dominion or international servicemen:

Rank	Name	Air Force	RAF Squadron
F/Lt	H. A. Picard	Belgian Air Force	350 (B)
F/Lt	A. Valenta	Czech Air Force	311
F/Lt	H. Birkland	Royal Canadian AF	72
F/Lt	P. W. Langford	Royal Canadian AF	16 OTU
F/Lt	G. E. McGill	Royal Canadian AF	103
F/Lt	J. C. Wernham	Royal Canadian AF	405
F/Lt	G. W. Wiley	Royal Canadian AF	112
F/O	G. A. Kidder	Royal Canadian AF	156
S/Ldr	J. Catanach, DFC	Royal Australian AF	455
F/Lt	R. V. Kierath	Royal Australian AF	450
W/O	A. H. Hake	Royal Australian AF	72
F/Lt	A. G. Christensen	Royal New Zealand AF	25
F/O	P. P. J. Pohe	Royal New Zealand AF	51
Lt	J. S. Gouws	South African AF	40
Lt	R. J. Stevens	South African AF	12
2nd Lt	F. C. McGarr	South African AF	2 SAAF
F/Lt	A. Kiewnarski	Polish Air Force	305 (P)
F/O	W. Kolanowski	Polish Air Force	301
F/O	J. T. Mondschein	Polish Air Force	304 (P)
F/O	K. Pawluk	Polish Air Force	305 (P)
F/O	S. Krol	Polish Air Force	74
F/O	P. Tobolski	Polish Air Force	301
2nd Lt	N. Fuglesang	Royal Norwegian AF	332 (N)
Sgt	H. Estelid	Royal Norwegian AF	331 (N)
Lt	B. W. H. Schneidhauer	French Air Force	131
W/O	E. Scantzikas	Royal Hellenic AF	336

Table 2: The twenty-six Dominion and international members of the RAF unlawfully executed following their escape from Stalag Luft III. (IX Squadron RAF historical records.)

Understandably, no black Caribbean or West African aircrew opted to join the attempt to escape and evade recapture by the Germans in the cold and grey of central Europe.

By January 1945 it was clear that the war in Europe was entering its final brutal phase. Cy Grant:

'It was to the east that we were looking for our salvation (as) the Russians were sweeping everything before them in a colossal drive …
The first visible signs of the proximity of the war came with the first bedraggled columns of the retreating German Army.'

The retreating German soldiers were accompanied by a gloomy, never-ending pilgrimage of misery and suffering – the civilian refugees from the eastern parts of the Reich. Some 500,000 of these would now swell the population of Dresden, just in time for the firestorm that would claim tens of thousands of lives.

The prisoners themselves were ordered to join the trek, pulling their possessions on makeshift wooden sledges through the snow in extreme cold and with no winter clothing. They trudged along on frozen feet, hungry, cold and fearful. Their guards, most of whom were older men, suffered almost as much as the prisoners themselves. The men endured a series of forced marches in deep snow for days on end as their German guards repeatedly moved them out of reach of the advancing Red Army. They did not know it at the time, but they were participating in 'The March' during which over 80,000 Allied PoWs, alongside the hundreds of thousands of German refugees, were forced to walk westwards and away from the Soviet lines.

The PoWs feared the worst. Many believed that they would now be taken to Nazi death camps and gassed or shot, as punishment for their role as 'terror fliers'. Others assumed that this was a deliberate death march, intended to kill them through hunger and exhaustion, along the lines of the infamous Japanese prisoner death marches that had taken place in Asia. A minority of the men thought that they would be used as a bargaining chip by the German government and later evidence suggested that there was merit to this theory.

'The March' took place during one of the coldest European winters on record, with temperatures dipping as low as -25° C and rarely going above zero degrees. Ill prepared and poorly clothed, with little to eat, sleeping in barns and then transported in cattle trucks, jammed together like sardines in a tin, some men who took part in this march were reduced to eating cats and dogs they caught on the way and the German guards often shot dead any prisoner who could not go on. At one point, Grant saw a group of Waffen SS combat troops, preparing to defend an area of dense forest:

'Dressed in their white winter uniforms, these were the creme-de-la-creme of the German Army; big, healthy-looking men, looking quite magnificent. They were deployed in the wood and took no notice of us straggling along in the snow. I looked at them apprehensively. They were fine specimens of Hitler's so-called master race alright, but you sensed that fate was catching up with them fast.'

Along the route, Grant's group found that the German population was generally friendly, trading hot water and bread for the cigarettes the prisoners held in abundance. War makes strange bedfellows and it also turns everyday items into valuable currency. Being lucky enough to hold a good stock of cigarettes, the new medium of exchange, made the difference between life and death for many PoWs.

Part of a retreating German Panzer Division now arrived with their tanks and halftracks. These troops were as friendly as the civilians had been and they too traded their food rations for coffee and cigarettes. The Panzertruppen acknowledged that their war was rapidly coming to an end and it seemed as though they were keen to make friends. They told the prisoners that it would all be over in a few days, which cheered the PoWs up, and everyone made small fires to heat their food and warm their bodies. A relaxed atmosphere then prevailed, disrupted only when the senior German officer discovered that a goose he was carrying in his vehicle had been stolen, killed, cooked and eaten by some anonymous British airmen. But even this hardened warrior of the eastern front was mollified by a compensatory gift of chocolate and American cigarettes.

Although the weather was now warming up, the PoWs hardships were far from over and neither was the war. The thaw turned the ground to mud and slush, adding to the misery of all, and with no Red Cross parcels to depend on now that they were on the march, the prisoners were receiving only a meagre German ration of a thin bowl of soup and a fifth of a loaf of bread each day. Hunger was now a bigger threat than the cold had been. As men started to drop out from the march, the British Medical Officer, who had somehow organized an oxcart, rescued the fallen in the wake of the column. In so doing, he may well have saved them from being shot by their guards.

By 3 February 1945, Grant's group of about two hundred airmen had reached Spremberg in south-eastern Germany and not far from the city of Dresden. Here they were finally given a thick serving of soup, marched to the train station and packed into cattle cars to be taken on a slow and tortuous journey to the Stalag III-A camp at Lukenwalde, Brandenburg, further to the north and quite close to Berlin. This was to be their final destination of the war.

Stalag III-A already held a large number of French troops, prisoners since 1940, and these included 4,000 black Africans from French colonial units, as well as another 4,000 American prisoners. It is interesting to note that the Nazis had allowed their black prisoners to live when millions of Soviet prisoners were deliberately starved to death, many in the same location as these African PoWs. Most of the 48,000 men held at the Lukenwalde camp were not actually housed in the main camp, but were distributed as slave labour throughout one thousand small forestry and agricultural work stations spread across the German state of Brandenburg.

Many of the black African prisoners had been selected to take part in the production of a very successful film, *Germanin: the Story of a Colonial Deed* (1943), which chronicled the battle against sleeping sickness and the conquest of the tsetse fly, one of the brighter chapters of German colonial history. Directed by Max Kimmich, the brother-in-law of Nazi Propaganda Minister Joseph Goebbels, the film also featured the black German actor Louis Brody, supported by a cast of 300 unpaid black French colonial prisoners.

Louis Brody was born M'bebe Mpessa in 1892, in the German colony of Kamerun, (now Cameroon). He died in Berlin in 1952 after a highly successful career in Germany as a notable black actor, musician, and wrestler. His career began in the 1920s and ran uninterrupted throughout the Nazi era, despite the demise of many of his black and Jewish friends. Brody was politically active on behalf of Afro-Germans under Hitler's rule, yet he remained an active and successful artist and his roles often emphasized the racial stigmas prevalent against blacks in Germany at the time. It is difficult to think of a more complicated and conflicted story; a Nazi-backed propaganda film involving a black German and focusing on Germany's commendable efforts to save Africans from disease, with the African roles being played by unpaid black PoW slave labourers. The film was made at a time in history when Germany was least disposed to show mercy to anyone who was not a member of the 'master race'.

The men remained at Stalag III-A, surviving in frozen, lice infected barrack rooms on their meagre rations, supplemented by those few Red Cross parcels that were still getting through to them and with none of the comforts of their earlier camp, which now seemed a pleasant place by comparison. Most of all, Grant missed the library.

Five thousand prisoners of war from seventeen nations are buried at Stalag III-A, although the great majority of these are Soviet dead, buried in a common grave. The other Allied dead are buried in individual graves, divided by nationality, a stark reminder of how ethnicity defined an individual's worth in that time and place.

The Germans had by now completed their metamorphosis from supermen to soon-to-be-vanquished foes and war criminals. This had only taken a few months and the prison guards had become exceedingly polite and obsequious towards their charges and were asking the PoWs for good conduct notes as evidence of their civilized behaviour. The Germans intended to show these to their own eventual captors, whom they prayed would be American, Canadian or British and not Russian. Many were to be disappointed as the Red Army was about to swarm past their camp on its way to Berlin.

On Sunday, 21 April, the Germans abandoned their guard posts and handed the camp over to the senior officer present, a Norwegian General named Otto Rude, a man who leaves the pages of history as abruptly as he enters them. The Germans then left in a chaotic rush, as the Red Army had suddenly appeared only a few miles to the south the day before. On the Monday, with sporadic fighting going on in the nearby town and in the woods all around the camp, the Russians arrived at the perimeter. Cy Grant:

> 'Six tanks and twenty-nine motorized units carrying Russian soldiers crashed through the camp, literally tearing down the perimeter fence amidst our cheers and excitement. Words cannot describe the scene. Our liberators were war-scarred fighting soldiers, a few women amongst them, flushed, wild-looking and armed to the teeth. We crowded around their tanks, cheering in joy, taken aback by the magnitude of the moment – feeling the barbarizm of war oozing from their bodies, their eyes, their entire demeanour. Free at last! Some Russian prisoners, who were strong enough, clambered aboard the tanks and were soon heading in the direction of Berlin.'

Following their liberation, danger continued to lurk in the woods bordering the compound. Small groups of German soldiers still held on and sniping was a problem. A group of German civilians ambushed and killed four former Russian prisoners. The killers were arrested and presumably executed soon after. Occasional strafing attacks by Luftwaffe aircraft also continued. Cy Grant:

> 'The Germans seemed prepared to fight the Russians to the death. They were well aware that the brutality and devastation they had unleashed on Russia would inevitably lead to reciprocal acts of barbarity upon themselves.'

After several false starts and much confusion and frustration, both Cy Grant and Johnny Smythe eventually made their separate ways safely back to England.

Chapter 9

Bombing the Reich

'Moral wounds have this peculiarity – they may be hidden, but they never close; always painful, always ready to bleed when touched, they remain fresh and open in the heart.'

Alexandre Dumas, The Count of Monte Cristo. Dumas, the famous French writer and thinker, was one quarter black, his paternal grandmother having been a slave woman in Saint-Domingue (Santo Domingo) and his grandfather a French nobleman.

A new RAF bomber crew on its first three missions was five times more likely to be killed than an experienced crew. With a five per cent loss rate per mission overall, this meant that new crews only had a forty per cent chance of surviving to fly their fourth mission. On a thirty mission tour, the statistical probability of death or capture was well above 100 per cent and RAF Bomber Command suffered, pro rata, the highest loss rate of any branch of the British Armed Forces during the war, although as the war in Europe drew to a close in the Spring of 1945, losses did decline.

Johnny Smythe described in his press interview what it was like to experience flak and enemy fighter attacks:

'We knew what lay ahead of us. Every day we counted the number that returned. We also knew that there was a good chance that we would not return. We met with our first serious trouble during an operation over Mainz in Germany. The plane had several times been pelted by flak and it was in a bad state. Although we lost one of our engines, we still managed to limp back home.

'On one occasion we were flying back over England when a German fighter began to dog us. I saw it first and yelled to the rear gunner, "Frank, open up!" It was quite scary because we were flying so low that, had the plane been actually shot down, we wouldn't have had time to bail out! The noise caused by the two aircraft brought our anti-aircraft fire from the ground, which fended off the German fighter, and we were able to land safely. Another lucky escape!'

John Ebanks, the Mosquito navigator, provided his own highlights when I interviewed him in 1997:

'All in all I flew fifty sorties during the war. I think my most dangerous moment was over Hamburg, my twenty-fourth trip. Intelligence had advised us that the Germans had installed anti-aircraft coverage with between 500 and 1,000 heavy guns. In due course, our aircraft received three hits, putting the starboard engine out of action. This occurred at 25,000 feet. Then suddenly the second engine packed up, apparently because of an airlock. So we were just gliding with no engines at all. By now we were over the North Sea and the pilot told me to prepare to bail out. I said "Mister, you can bail out, but I am not bailing out." This was one time I was not obeying any instructions, because when you looked down below it was as black as pitch, it being two o'clock in the morning. There was no way in hell I was going to bail out at night, in the winter, over the North Sea – I would prefer to die in my plane. When we got to 5,000 feet the blockage cleared up, the engine started and we were able to land on an emergency strip on the east coast of England. You see, no matter how bad things get, there is always a chance something will happen and you will scrape through. I just wasn't prepared to bail out because you had no chance of surviving; you would freeze to death in two minutes in the water.'

John Ebanks also recalled another occasion when his aircraft lost an engine and they had to turn back to base prematurely, aborting the mission. Each squadron leaving Britain had a designated re-entry point at which it was safe to fly back in. As long as they flew on the correct course they would be expected, but if they returned on another route there was a good chance that British anti-aircraft gunners on the ground would regard them as a likely enemy aircraft. As John's plane hit the coast the English anti-aircraft batteries opened fire. Fortunately the aircrews always carried a Very pistol with the flare of the day, this being a specific colour that everyone on the ground had been told about. As soon as he fired his flare the anti-aircraft firing stopped as though by magic.

Between 2 and 22 January 1945, John Blair's crew flew another six missions (Ops V to Ops X) dropping their bombs on Ludwigshafen, where they destroyed the IG Farben chemical works (amongst other things, this company had produced the gas used in the Nazi extermination camps); Hanau, where the wind scattered their bombs over a wide area of the city; Saarbruken railway yards, which were hit accurately; Dulmen Luftwaffe fuel storage depot, where the bombs landed in open fields; the city of Magdeburg, which was subjected to saturation bombing and Gelsenkirchen once again, where both residential and industrial zones were targeted.

John's crew did not fly on 5 January, but the squadron did attack Hannover that night and had a rough time, losing three aircraft, with seventeen men killed and six taken prisoner. At least one of the 102 Squadron aircraft was shot down by a night fighter piloted by Luftwaffe Hauptman Georg-Hermann Greiner, who shot down a total of four RAF bombers in only ten minutes, the other three being Lancasters.

On the Magdeburg run, on 16 January, the aircraft's compasses stopped working, and John Blair had to navigate without them, which was quite a challenge, but he got them home in one piece using plain old map-reading. The RAF suffered heavy losses during this attack, which also destroyed forty per cent of the city. Altogether, seventeen Halifax aircraft were lost, representing 5.3 per cent of the attacking force.

The loss of Halifax LW179DY-Y, flown by Squadron Leader Jarand, brought the total number of men killed in 102 Squadron to twenty-nine in just four weeks. Nevertheless, although they did not know it then, they were through the worst. In the last months of the war 102 Squadron would only lose another five aircraft. Other squadrons were less fortunate and continued to lose men and aircraft right up to the end of the war in Europe, in May 1945.

On 29 January 1945, John Blair headed for Stuttgart on Ops XI. This time the bomb load 'hung up', meaning that the bombs wouldn't release and the crew had to release them manually. This was a terrifying task at twenty thousand feet, the frightened men working feverishly to release the deadly cargo with the bomb doors open below them, no safety harnesses to hold them should they slip and fall, and the screaming dark rushing by beneath their feet at 250 miles per hour. Finally, on hands and knees and reaching down into the bomb bay to work the release gear, they got the bombs away and they landed at RAF Tangmere, every nerve jangling. A combination of cloud, dummy target indicator rockets set off by the Germans, hilly terrain and dummy target fires, meant that the bombing had been very scattered in this final RAF raid against Stuttgart and casualties on the ground were relatively light as a result.

The men continued to feel as though a great weight had been lifted off them each time the bombs were released. They still had flak and fighters to face, but at least they were rid of all the explosives they had been carrying. There was a collective sigh of relief when they reached this point in the mission and the whole mindset of the crews was to get the bombs to the target as quickly as possible and then get rid of them before making a quick about face. Getting home in one piece was at the forefront of their minds and what they were doing with their bomb loads was sanctioned at the highest levels, where strategic matters were better understood, and therefore not to be questioned by a crew with an average age of about twenty-five.

And so the sequence repeated itself, one, two, three nights each week, weather permitting, through thirty fear filled, flak plastered, fighter intercepted missions. On 2 February, 102 Squadron's bombing was again frustrated by cloud as they attacked the oil refinery at Wanne Eickel. There was the usual crack of flak going off around them, and then John and his crew heard a sudden louder bang and the aircraft was shaken violently. Their starboard outer engine died immediately and they lost altitude before the pilot was able to regain control and level the aircraft. The crew had been bracing themselves for the worst, but they flew home on three engines.

A mission over Bonn followed on the night of 5 February and they then had a tough time with the flak over Goch on 7/8 February, their Op XIV. The anti-aircraft fire was always extremely unpleasant, but the crews soon learned that they had no choice but to live with it. On most missions, their commanders would attempt to route them around known enemy flak concentrations, so that their route through the air to the target would depend as much on the position of the enemy gunners on the ground as on anything else. But many of the guns were mobile and the Germans would switch locations so that at least some of their fire simply could not be escaped. In those circumstances the aircraft had to fly on through the shell bursts and hope for the best. Of course, there was always plenty of flak surrounding the target. John Blair:

'We knew that wherever the target was, it was going to be loaded with flak. Once we got there we just had to say, "Well, here goes!" and head into it.'

The Germans had included the towns of Goch and Kleve in their strong defences near the Reichswald frontier. The Goch raid involved 464 aircraft and was intended to prepare the way for the attack of the British army. The Master Bomber ordered the raid to come in below the cloud and as the cloud base was at only 5,000ft the attack was very accurate at first. However, the raid was stopped after 155 aircraft had bombed because smoke was causing control of the raid to become impossible. Blair's crew did not bomb for this reason, but their course still took them straight through the smoke and directly over the target and its defenders. Two more Halifax aircraft from the squadron were lost on this raid. The first was shot down by a Luftwaffe night fighter and all seven crew died. The second was also attacked by a fighter aircraft and the Captain, Warrant Officer Smith, ordered the crew to bail out. Six of them did so safely and they returned to Pocklington soon after, but Smith himself was unable to escape and he burned to death in the crash.

On 21 February, while hitting the city of Worms, of which thirty-nine per cent was destroyed during the only major attack it suffered throughout the war, John Blair's crew had a memorable tangle with German fighters which made repeated passes, spraying cannon fire at the plane. Several of these German aircraft infiltrated to the heart of the British formation and made good their attacks and twenty-five RAF bombers were shot down over various parts of Germany that night, eight of them aircraft taking part in the Worms mission. Luftwaffe Ace Hauptmann Greiner was again active in the air on this night, shooting down two of the RAF bombers, and three other German aces flew in the same area; Gunther Bahr, Heinz Schnaufer and Heinz Rökker. Between them, these four men accounted for twenty-four of the twenty-five bombers downed.

The bomber crews rarely had such prolonged engagements with the enemy fighter pilots. The fighters would come in fast and try and get in close, but the RAF gunners were well trained and the enemy would generally be chased off after one or two passes. Once a fighter pilot realized that the crew in the bomber was alert and aggressive, he was unlikely to press forward in the face of heavy machine-gun fire.

Good navigation was also a very important factor in this defence. If a bomber could stay on course it would have the company of many other aircraft, with all the tail gunners and top gunners in the vicinity firing simultaneously at any intruder, increasing the collective odds of survival. This was one of the main reasons why the more experienced crews had better survival rates – it was generally the novices who got lost or separated from the pack. Every crew needed steady nerves, great teamwork and lightning reflexes to survive and the weak, wayward, or downright unlucky paid with their lives.

The month of February 1945 came to a close for 102 Squadron with attacks on the huge Krupps armaments works at Essen, where the Germans recorded that the bombers were very accurate, dropping 300 high explosive bombs and 11,000 incendiaries directly on the target. The squadron also made an attack on the synthetic oil plant at Kamen. In the final week of that month they were upgraded to the Halifax VI bomber, which had better engines and a longer range, and on 25 February, John Blair's crew flew cross-country to familiarize themselves with their new aircraft.

They returned to Cologne for a third time for Ops XIX on 2 March 1945. This was a daylight raid and the Allied front line had almost reached it, but the city was still defended by over four hundred flak guns. Cologne had already taken a terrible hammering on previous raids and the damage was very extensive. There was almost nothing left in the centre of Cologne, but the bombs were dropped once more and the crews reported 'spectacular fires and large explosions'. The river and urban areas, which had been clearly visible as the planes arrived over the target, were completely hidden by smoke and dust a few minutes later as they departed. The city fell to American troops four days later, to the certain relief of most of its surviving inhabitants.

Another trip to Kamen at the eastern end of the Ruhr the following night hit the synthetic oil plant without loss to the attackers, taking the facility out of production for the remainder of the conflict. By this stage, Germany was on its last legs and shortages of oil had already crippled the war effort. Raids like this one represented the final nail in the coffin.

The return trip from Kamen saw John Blair's aircraft being hit by intruders once again, this time as they crossed the English coast. The Luftwaffe, which clearly had no intention of giving up without a struggle, had adopted an aggressive new tactic that involved attacking bombers close to their bases as they were preparing to land, and on this first occasion it caught the crew completely by surprise. Once again, they were forced to fly home on three engines.

In the week that followed, 102 Squadron flew in raids that struck Chemnitz and they dropped sea mines in Flemsberg Fjord. The Chemnitz raid required them to take off in icy conditions, and another participating squadron lost several aircraft due to mid-air collisions. This target was to be another Dresden. It was a rail and road hub, close to the advancing Russian front and also flooded with refugees. Some men felt ill at the thought of once again deliberately bombing civilians, but most had by now become hardened to the reality of the war and regarded what they were engaged in as simply doing their jobs. Theirs was not to reason why.

John Blair felt that he was lucky to be a navigator – even at this late stage in his tour he was still too busy to be frightened. But there were others on the crew who were not busy enough and they suffered dearly. Blair later said that he would not have wanted to be sitting all alone in the tail of the aircraft as a tail gunner, waiting for a night fighter to come in and take potshots at him. Nor would he have liked to have been a pilot, trying to hold the aircraft straight and level while flying into flak, able to see everything that was coming up at him but unable to do anything about it. With the plane twisting and turning and with all the pressure to be accurate in his navigation, he was simply too busy to worry about anything else. The formations never seemed to fly in the same direction for more than fifty miles and every five minutes or so they would turn left or turn right, descend or ascend, in order to make sure that the enemy could not train their guns on them effectively, or predict their next move. As a result, a navigator was always just three or four minutes from the next turn and working like a madman to get everything ready.

By now, Bomber Command's 'heavies' were flying an increasing number of daylight missions, as their American counterparts had been doing from the outset, although major night raids also continued. The RAF crews flying by day could at last see where they were going and where the other aircraft in the bomber stream were. But daylight also meant that they were exposed to attack from the new German jet aircraft, one of Hitler's 'wonder weapons', which were intended to turn the tide of war in Germany's favour. On occasions, the vapour trails left by German V2 rockets, heading for England, were also clearly visible in the blue skies of Western Europe.

In one attack, John Blair's squadron struck the shipyards in Hamburg on 8 March, in a raid designed to delay the production of new long-range German U-boats. These Type XXI boats were equipped with a snorkel device that allowed them to stay submerged for very long periods of time and had the war lasted much longer, they would have represented a dangerous new threat to Allied shipping and logistics. The bomber crews could not see the target clearly, but they reported one huge explosion on the ground lasting ten to fifteen seconds. The exact cause was not known.

On 11 March 1945, Blair took part in the last thousand bomber raid on Essen. Essen was a major target in the heart of the Ruhr, Germany's industrial centre, and large raids had headed this way repeatedly over several years. On this raid, 1,079 aircraft of all bomber groups attacked Essen, making it the largest air raid so far in the war. Three Lancaster aircraft from other squadrons were lost during the attack, but 4,661 tons of bombs were dropped through complete cloud cover. Although the bomber crews could see nothing of the ground, a huge black mushroom cloud pushed its way upwards through the clouds. Essen was already in ruins before the attack and later reports confirmed that the attack was accurate and that this blow virtually paralyzed Essen until American troops entered the city some time later. During the war, 7,000 people had died in the air raids on this city and the pre-war population of 648,000 had fallen to

310,000 by the end of the war, as most of the other inhabitants had left for safer places in Germany.

No. 102 Squadron then took part in attacks on Wuppertal, Bottrop and Witten between the 13 and 19 March. The flak over Bottrop on 15 March was very bad and one Halifax was shot down from another squadron. In the Witten raid the bombers destroyed 129 acres of the city, or sixty-two per cent, consisting of both industrial and residential districts. The industrialization of the strategic bombing campaign was now complete and RAF Bomber Command had been turned into an awesome weapon of mass annihilation – a city killer. At the end of March, John Blair had two dream missions over Dulmen and Osnabruck with almost no enemy action being observed. However, the crew again lost an engine due to technical problems on 25 March and had to return from Osnabruck on three engines, but they were getting used to that by this stage. Both of these operations were daytime area attacks and the men could see large fires and lots of dust and smoke as they flew away from the targets.

Chapter 10

A Full Tour

To survive a single tour, all RAF aircrew had to complete thirty operational missions. The statistical chances of survival were low, well below zero for those commencing their tours in 1943 or mid-1944 and not much better for those joining later. After completing such a tour, each man was entitled to a period of rest, following which a further tour of twenty missions was required. Anyone who survived this second tour was then moved to training duties as an instructor, or to other non-combat roles, with the exception of those who volunteered to return to operational flying. A surprising number did.

With only four missions to go to complete his first thirty mission tour, John Blair was counting down and praying hard. Men had been known to make it through twenty-nine operations without a scratch, only to be blasted out of the sky on their final outing. The crew returned to Hamburg for the last time on 8 April 1945, to attack the shipyards and U-boat pens once more. Another three Halifax and three Lancaster aircraft were shot down that night, but this also turned out to be the final RAF raid on the city. The following night John's squadron again dropped mines into the Flemsburg Fjord. They met no opposition and every plane returned home safely.

On 13 April they bombed Nuremberg, site of the Nazi Party rallies and the future site of the Nazi war crimes trials. This city had special significance for John Blair as a black person. He had seen footage of the huge Nazi rallies that were held there, and knew of the discriminatory German race laws that were created in the name of the city during the 1930s. To be flying in one of the aircraft assigned to bomb the city made him think about the long, arduous and dangerous journey he had taken to get there.

Finally, on 18 April 1945, John Blair of Jamaica flew his last mission of the war. On this final mission his crew was part of a force that attacked a heavily fortified island off Germany's north-west coast, named Heligoland. This bastion literally bristled with heavy guns and concrete emplacements. John recalled that this was a 'hell of a prang', as he put it in RAF parlance. 'The island was armed and defended like no other place in the world, but we gave them a hammering'. The attack was made in daylight and the force carried the very heavy Blockbuster bombs designed to pierce the thick ceilings of the enemy bunkers. RAF fighter-bomber aircraft also attacked with rockets to suppress the German anti-aircraft positions. Despite the weight of the attack, another three Halifax aircraft were lost on this raid.

On this final raid, after dropping their bombs, the crew did something they had never dared do before and they circled the target watching the explosions caused by the bombs dropped by aircraft that had flown in behind them. They saw huge secondary explosions caused by munitions or fuel on the ground being hit. They knew that there was nothing left down there to touch them and there was not a single gun firing back, only huge clouds of smoke.

Twenty-five per cent of the Caribbean volunteer aircrew were decorated for their actions between 1941 and 1945. One representative example was Harold Cherberd Bryant, from Dominica, who served with 514 Squadron and was awarded the DFC for his actions. The Air Ministry Citation, dated 21 April 1944, reads:

'The KING has been graciously pleased to approve the following award, in recognition of gallantry displayed in flying operations against the enemy: Distinguished Flying Cross. Flying Officer Harold Cherberd BRYANT (143598), RAFVR 514 Squadron. This officer was the mid-upper gunner of an aircraft detailed to attack Frankfurt in March 1944. Whilst on the bombing run the windscreen on the starboard side of his turret was shattered. An article of stores was seen to be on fire close to an ammunition tank. The danger was averted by Flying Officer Bryant, however, who acted with great promptitude and ejected the burning article through the broken windscreen. Although his turret could not be rotated mechanically, while the windscreen was shattered, Flying Officer Bryant insisted on manning the position and remained alert to the possibility of fighter interference. His oxygen tube had been severed by flying splinters, but he resourcefully maintained his supply by holding the severed ends together. This officer displayed great courage, fortitude and devotion to duty.'

John Blair's unit, No. 102 (Ceylon) Squadron, suffered the third heaviest overall losses of any Bomber Command Squadron during the Second World War, losing 192 aircraft in total, with an average loss rate of three per cent per operation. Of the 125,000 men who served as aircrew in Bomber Command, 47,268 were killed on operations, or died while being held as prisoners of war. Another 8,195 aircrew were killed in accidents, many of those during training, and a further thirty-seven died during battle action on the ground. The total loss of 55,500 killed represents sixty per cent of all those who flew operationally, or forty-four per cent of the whole force. When the wounded are added, the total casualties exceed eighty per cent of the entire force. Today, when the loss of a single RAF aircraft on operations, or on a training flight is a disaster for the nation, it is hard for anyone who did not live through the war to comprehend the magnitude of the sacrifice made by all who fought, willingly or otherwise, to create the conditions of freedom and relative prosperity that we now enjoy.

John Blair had completed thirty-three operational missions by 18 April 1945, about three weeks before the war itself ended in Europe:

'After I finished my tour it was time for us to go and get drunk! It was a big relief to come through it all alive, yet I am sure that if the war had continued I would have signed up for another tour of duty straightaway. I can't really explain why. It's something to do with the way I felt at the time – that we were doing the right thing, and that it was important.

'There were people who went up for their operational first flight and then decided that they weren't ready for this at all, that they were not going back in the air. I have to admit that I believe what we did was something most people would not be able to do in the same circumstances. Without meaning to sound conceited, I believe that the process of selection and the intensive period of training brought a special group of people to the top of the pile.'

Ralph Pearson, one air gunner and John Blair, all volunteered to join the RAF's elite Pathfinder Force. Their applications were approved and they were posted to the Pathfinder training school to train on the Lancaster bomber. However, after about two weeks of this familiarization training the Germans surrendered and the war in Europe came to a close. Blair was now posted to 35 Squadron, which flew Lancaster bombers, where he remained until October 1947, before becoming an RAF navigation instructor at RAF Scampton.

With the end of the conflict in Europe, Blair's pilot, Pearson, just disappeared. Blair tried to contact him before he left for Canada, but the Canadians were taken home very quickly by their government. Pearson was engaged to a girl in York, England and with very little time left to him, he rushed off to join her about three days before the formal end of the fighting, while Blair was still stuck at the Pathfinder training centre awaiting orders. As soon as he was able, Blair hopped onto the first train to York, but try as he might he couldn't find Pearson. He visited everybody who knew the pilot, trying to get some information about his whereabouts, but the search was in vain. Eventually Blair gave up, and, as he could not find a room in a hotel anywhere due to the great influx of servicemen and women flooding back from overseas, he ended up spending the whole depressing night sitting in York railway station. The next day he caught the first train back to his base and he never saw or heard from Ralph Pearson again. The pilot had left so abruptly that the two men had not even exchanged postal addresses.

His failure to track down his respected pilot, a man who had ignored his skin colour and had chosen him for his crew, troubled John Blair deeply. In 1959 he travelled to Vancouver with the RAF as a navigator in the new Comet aircraft. This was the city in which Pearson had lived before the war and while Blair was there he wrote to several addresses in an attempt to contact him, but once again he could find no sign of the man. John Blair never found out whether Ralph Pearson eventually married the girl from Yorkshire and what turns his life might have taken thereafter. He was still wondering about it when I interviewed him in 1997, fifty-two years on.

John Blair did stay in touch with Laurie Wilder, the flight engineer. Wilder worked in the Middle East for many years but died after his eventual return to England. Of the others in the crew, Blair only met one man after the war:

'I was walking along a street in London when I heard someone walking behind me. I knew it was a policeman but I didn't worry about that as I knew he was just going to walk past me. Suddenly, this policeman turned around to face me and said, "Excuse me, sir". I thought he was going to arrest me, but as it turned out it was Morris, one of the mid-upper gunners, who had now joined the police force.

'I exclaimed, "My God!" I had had a shock you know, because when you hear "Excuse me, sir", from a policeman, you know that the next words coming are, "You are wanted for questioning down at the Station"!'

John Blair remained with the RAF after the war. One day in late 1945, returning from a Transport Command trip to the Middle East, he climbed down from his aircraft and saw three or four staff cars and a gaggle of senior officers waiting beside the runway. The Wing Commander, who was at the head of the group, called out, 'John Blair, come here!'

John walked over, trying to work out what kind of trouble he was in, when the Wing Commander handed him something and said, 'This is yours! You've been awarded the Distinguished Flying Cross! Well done!'

And John replied, 'What for?' That reaction sums up the man.

John Blair:

'Of course, the night after they gave me the medal was a terrible night! From whiskey to beer to whiskey and back again! Beer by the barrel-full and whiskey by the bottle, even though money was tight. I really couldn't afford that medal.'

John flew all over the world as a navigator in Hastings and Comet aircraft. He met his future wife Margaret, who was the Senior Flight (nursing) Sister, on an aircraft flying into Hong Kong to collect casualties suffered during the British post-war counter-insurgency campaign in Malaya, now Malaysia. A few years later, he was based in the middle of the Pacific Ocean, dropping off cargo destined for Christmas Island in the period leading up to the British nuclear tests. His career with the RAF lasted until 1963 when he returned to Jamaica, taking Margaret and their two young children with him.

Chapter 11

Forgotten Warriors

'There yet remains but one concluding tale, and then this chronicle of mine is ended.'

Alexander Pushkin, Eugene Onegin (1823).
Pushkin was a prominent Russian writer and poet whose great-grandfather was Abram Petrovich Gannibal (1696–1781), a black African page from Ethiopia, raised by the Russian Tsar, Peter the Great.

As the decades passed, the contribution and sacrifices of the Caribbean RAF volunteers were forgotten by all but a tiny few. In the wake of national independence in each of the former British colonies it quickly became unfashionable to identify with the imperial era and many expressed outright contempt for those who had fought for the Empire. The fate of their Luftwaffe opponents, also human beings, has remained a topic that is rarely discussed outside Germany, although following the period of de-nazification in Germany, large numbers of those men served for many years with NATO forces during the Cold War.

Johnny Smythe

After the war, Smythe worked at the Colonial Office helping Commonwealth servicemen and he also studied at the Inns of Court School of Law in London. He was called to the Bar, at Middle Temple, in 1951. Later that same year he married Violet Wells Bain, with whom he would have five children, and he transferred to the RAF reserve. Smythe eventually returned to Sierra Leone where he continued his law career. He was commissioned into the Sierra Leone Naval Volunteer Force and he represented that service at the coronation of Queen Elizabeth II in 1953. Smythe continued to prosper in his homeland, and having become a Queen's Counsel, he was appointed the country's Attorney-General. He was awarded an OBE in 1978. He eventually returned to Britain, retiring to the town of Thame, in Oxfordshire, where he died in 1996 at the age of eighty-one.

Ulric Cross

Ulric Cross earned the distinction of becoming one of the most decorated of the Caribbean aircrew, receiving both the DSO and the DFM, ending the war as a Squadron Leader. Cross was then sent to the Colonial Office to act as liaison for all colonial forces. It was there that he was phoned and advised that he was awarded the DSO. A plane was sent for him and he was given the award and there was a party. Cross said:

> 'I (initially) flew thirty missions over Germany and occupied Europe. After thirty missions one earns a rest and can divert to teaching other pilots etc. However, I was interested in continuing the mission. At fifty missions, they again asked me to take a rest. I declined and flew eighty missions over Germany and occupied Europe before the war ended. I did twenty-two missions over Berlin and made it through much flak; but one had to focus on the mission.'

Cross later served as a Judge in Ghana, Cameroon, Tanzania and Trinidad and as Ambassador of Trinidad and Tobago to Germany, France and Norway. He was also Trinidad's High Commissioner to the UK. At the time of my research and as late as 2012, Cross was still active as a writer and commentator on his home island of Trinidad. He sadly passed away in October 2013.

Orville Lynch

After speaking with Orville Lynch's son in 2005 by telephone, I learned that Lynch had returned to Jamaica, but later made his home in New York, USA. However, he was unable to take phone calls or to give interviews.

4122 Supplement to the *London Gazette*, 5 September 1944
605500 Flight Sergeant Lincoln Orville Lynch, RAF, 102 Sqn

'As air gunner, Flight Sergeant Lynch has taken part in a large number of sorties and has displayed a high standard of determination and devotion to duty throughout. He has defended his aircraft with great skill on several occasions against enemy fighters, one of which he shot down on his first sortie. His conduct has at all times been exemplary and he has proved himself to be a worthy member of a fine crew.'

Orville Lynch was later commissioned as a Flight Lieutenant, becoming one of only a handful of RAF air gunners to hold an officer rank.

Vincent Bunting

Having flown fighter aircraft through the better part of the war, in April 1945, Bunting was commissioned as a Pilot Officer and in June that year he received his last flying posting, joining the prestigious No. 1 Squadron, RAF. Subsequently, Vincent Bunting served in administrative posts prior to being discharged from the RAF with the rank of Flight Lieutenant in 1948. His later fate is so far un-established.

Arthur Wint

Known as the 'Gentle Giant', Flight Lieutenant Arthur Stanley Wint, who had served operationally during the war as a pilot, left the RAF in 1947. Wint became the first Jamaican Olympic gold medallist, winning the 400m sprint at the 1948 Summer Olympics in London. Four years later, in Helsinki, he was part of the historic Jamaican team that set a new world record as it captured gold in the 4 x 400m relay. Wint had previously been the Jamaica Boy Athlete of the year in 1937 and the 800m gold medallist at the Central American Games in Panama in 1938. He also set a Canadian 400m record while training in Canada in the early 1940s. Anywhere in the world Wint arrived, records were destined to fall.

From 1947, Wint attended St Bartholomew's Hospital as a medical student. In 1953 he ran his final race at Wembley Stadium, finished his internship, graduated as a doctor and the following year he was made a Member of the British Empire (MBE) by Queen Elizabeth II.

In 1955, Wint returned to Jamaica and eventually settled in Hanover as the only resident doctor in that Parish at that time. In 1973 he was awarded the Jamaican honour, The Order of Distinction and he then served as Jamaica's High Commissioner to Britain from 1974 to 1978. Wint was inducted into the US Black Athlete's Hall of Fame in 1977, the Jamaica Sports Hall of Fame in 1989 and the Central American & Caribbean Athletic Confederation Hall of Fame in 2003. Arthur Wint died in October 1992 at the age of seventy-two.

Billy Strachan
Although Billy Strachan survived the war, I have been unable to find any information about his subsequent life or career.

Cy Grant
Speaking to the *Daily Telegraph* newspaper many years after the war, Cy Grant said:

> 'We need to acknowledge the past. The memorial for the 55,000 men of Bomber Command who died is needed because, unless we are informed by the past, we will not be able to make a better future for all mankind. In Bomber Command, 6,000 ground crew and (over) 400 aircrew were from the Caribbean. Over 100 (of the latter) were decorated. Those men who died were fighting for peace. I would like to see a memorial that isn't viewed as a war memorial, but as a peace memorial.'

Cy Grant qualified as a Barrister but, unable to find a place in Chambers in the UK, he became a successful television personality, appearing in numerous films and TV shows. The story of his last mission is told in *Lancaster W4827: failed to return*, by Joost Klootwijk, who lived near the crash site and saw one engine of Grant's aircraft hit a farmhouse near his home. Cy Grant passed away in 2010.

Lawrence (Larry) Osborne
Despite not previously appearing in this story (he flew as a Coastal Command navigator during the war), Osborne, who was from Trinidad, deserves a special mention because he later became the first black RAF Group Captain.

Serving as an air traffic controller in the RAF after the war, he retired in 1977 and passed away in 1995, aged seventy-three. Larry Osborne is the highest ranking non-white Caribbean volunteer of the Second World War that I have been able to identify.

John Blair

The award of John Blair's Distinguished Flying Cross was published in the *London Gazette* of Tuesday, 4 December 1945, but he remained in the RAF until 1963 and he had many more tales to tell of his post-war experiences, which accounted for eighteen of his twenty-one years' RAF service. John Blair engaged in experimental high altitude bombing work at Martlesham Heath in Suffolk in 1950 and in November of that year he was posted to the Colonial Office, where he was tasked with looking after the interests of colonial servicemen in the Army and Air Force. In parallel with his RAF career, he studied law, joined the Middle Temple Inn of Court and was called to the English Bar in April 1954.

In August 1954, John was posted to Transport Command and he regularly flew to the Middle East and the Far East, including Australia, Japan and Hong Kong. He was involved in transport flights to Christmas Island during Britain's highly controversial nuclear tests, conducted between 1956 and 1958. In 1957, the piston engined aircraft were replaced by the De Havilland Comet and in 1959 John was appointed Chief Navigation Officer of 216 Squadron, flying Comets until 1961 when he was posted to the Air Training School. He left the RAF and returned home to Jamaica in 1963, where he joined the Jamaica Bar Association and served as Deputy Clerk of Court for the Parish of Clarendon. In June 1966 he returned to aviation as the Deputy Director of Civil Aviation, Jamaica. He later acted as Director of Civil Aviation from 1975 to 1979 when he retired. He continued to serve, when required, as Jamaica's Inspector of Air Accidents while also running a small legal practice in the town of May Pen.

In 1995 John Blair was invited to represent Jamaica at the 50th Anniversary celebrations of the end of the war, held in London. Several former members of RAF aircrew represented Jamaica, including his close friend John Ebanks. John Blair said later that the event was quite something; it was very well attended and he had never before seen the streets of London so packed. The veterans marched from Greenwich to Buckingham Palace and people were standing more than twenty deep on both sides of the street all the way to the Palace. It felt to him as though there were millions of people present on that day:

> 'While I was fighting I never thought about defending the British Empire or anything else along those lines. I just knew deep down inside that we were all in this together and that what was taking place around our world had to be stopped. That was a war that had to be fought; there were no two ways about that. A lot of people have never thought about what would have happened to them in Jamaica if the Germans had won, but we certainly would have returned to slavery. If a youngster today should ever suggest that we had no business going to fight a "white man's war" I would just kick him where it hurts the most!'

John J. Blair, DFC, died in Jamaica in 2004, aged eighty-five, after a prolonged illness throughout which he was nursed by his devoted wife, Margaret. His first operational aircraft, NA 615 'Z', survived the war, but was struck off charge on 7 October 1946 and scrapped.

Citation (DFC) 1945, Flying Officer John J. Blair

> 'Flying Officer BLAIR, a navigator, has completed a full tour of Operations with Bomber Command comprising thirty-three sorties (198 hours flying). During his tour he has operated against such German targets as Cologne, Essen, Magdeburg, Chemnitz and Hamburg. He has also taken part in sea mining.
>
> 'At all times he has proved himself to be a skilful navigator and has obtained some very good results, especially in sea mining. His keenness and devotion to duty has been always of the highest standard and although he has experienced rather arduous conditions, on several occasions, his determination and skill in navigating his aircraft has enabled the crew to bomb the target on every possible occasion.

'Once, the bombs had to be released manually whilst the aircraft was orbiting the target and later in his tour it became necessary to feather the starboard inner engine one hour before reaching the target, but by dogged determination and skilful navigation the crew were able to bomb the target at 3,000 feet below the flight planned height.

'I consider this navigator's operational skill and devotion to duty fully merit for him the award of the DFC.'

Harry McCalla

Harry McCalla remained in England after the war and in 1969 he featured in a book titled *The Eighth Passenger*, by Miles Tripp, which tells the story of their crew of seven in Lancaster A-Able of 218 Squadron. The eighth passenger was fear. Miles was the bomb aimer and Harry was the tail gunner. When asked by Tripp whether the war and the Bomber Command campaign were worth the cost in objective terms, McCalla replied forcefully:

'Worth it? Of course it was! No question of it. It would have been ten times worse today if Britain had lost the war.'

McCalla was passionate about individual rights and liberties. He may have joined up for the adventure, but he left the RAF convinced that the rights of every individual to express his views freely and without fear are sacrosanct. For Harry McCalla, freedom of speech was a transcendental freedom and one worth a fight to the death to protect.

John Ebanks

After the war Flight Lieutenant John Ebanks also joined RAF Transport Command. He then accepted a short service commission as a Welfare Officer for West Indian airmen stationed at RAF Benson in Oxfordshire. John finally returned to Jamaica in 1953, where he continued to work tirelessly for the welfare and support of Jamaican ex-servicemen and women, many of whom barely got by on their limited pensions.

John Ebanks did not find the adjustment to life back home a challenge, even after a decade away, but he did have a very difficult time finding a job.

At every interview John attended, he was told that he had a brilliant war record, but that they had no place for someone of his calibre. He eventually found employment, married and raised a family. In 2000, burglars entered John's home in Kingston and removed all of his medals, RAF photo albums and other memorabilia.

John Ebanks was attending a formal gathering in Jamaica, shortly before I interviewed him in the late 1990s, when a young man came up to him and said sarcastically, 'Oh, so you are one of those who went to fight for "King and Country" are you?' John got very angry and responded forcefully that he had not gone to fight for King and Country; he had gone to fight for himself.

'I went to fight for freedom, for Jamaica, and for all the little countries of the world that would otherwise be controlled by bullies.'

John died in November 2004. His stolen medals and treasured photograph albums were never recovered.

Epilogue

D uring my research I was very fortunate to come into contact with the entertaining and articulate Wing Commander Jez Holmes, MA, who at the time of writing in 2013, is the Officer Commanding II (AC) Squadron RAF, the first RAF squadron to have flown fixed wing aircraft – as Jez immediately informed me upon meeting him at a Burns night dinner that year. No. 1 Squadron initially operated balloons and no doubt they are frequently reminded of that dark secret.

The Burns dinner was held at RAF Marham, the station from which the Trinidadian volunteer Ulric Cross had flown during the war. As I was in the final stages of my research, I naturally asked Jez whether he knew of Cross and the other Caribbean volunteers. To my amazement, not only did he know of them, but when studying for his MA, he had written his thesis on the subject of the Dominion contribution and this very topic had captured his imagination. I couldn't believe my luck as Jez gave me his own animated account of what these exceptional individuals had done.

Jez kindly consented to share his work with me and several of the statistics and other observations in this book, including key quotes by Cy Grant, Johnny Smythe and Billy Strachan, were first seen by me in Jez's thesis work. Equally valuable were the insights I gained into the workings of today's Royal Air Force when Jez invited me to visit his unit at Marham. The high esteem in which the wing commander was held by his officers was very evident and the character and manner of those fine men and women has obvious roots in the spirit of 'The Few'. Indeed, with today's budgetary restrictions, 'The Few' is once again an apt description. These dedicated, resolute professionals put their lives at risk for our collective security on a daily basis and they are deserving of the very best support and equipment that our nation can offer.

Cy Grant's book, however, included some observations about the attitudes of some very influential men at the top of the RAF in 1944–45 that shook me. In mid 1944, with the war seemingly almost won, the active recruitment of Caribbean and West African black and coloured volunteers was discontinued. Both the RAF and the Air Ministry proposed the reinstatement of the 'pure European descent' requirement for officer candidates. Their argument was that 'in the rough and tumble of wartime' the use of multi-racial crews had worked, but that once the service returned to its normal post-war rhythm, this practice would become increasingly problematic. However, the Colonial Office now put its foot down, stating that any attempt to reimpose the colour bar would be 'flatly contrary to the avowed policy of His Majesty's Government' and further stating that black men had shown themselves fully capable of serving and fighting as officers in wartime and that it was therefore impossible to ever again consider them as unsuitable to hold similar positions in peacetime.

The Air Ministry gave the appearance of bowing to this logic, but in fact implemented an unofficial policy of discrimination, whereby black candidates were permitted to apply, but most selection boards were 'verbally instructed as to the course they should pursue', which was to 'eliminate them'. The Ministry stated that, 'the application of this unwritten rule (would) require great tact and diplomacy'.

Nevertheless, on 19 November 1945, the Secretary of State for Air, Viscount Stansgate, triumphantly informed the Secretary of State for the Colonies that the Air Council had decided not to reintroduce the colour bar 'in the form in which it existed before the war…' He appears to have written this in good faith, believing that the bar would not now be reinstated, whether officially or unofficially.

However, all was not as it seemed and a memorandum dated 16 August 1945 that had been penned by Air Chief Marshal Sir John C. Slessor, Air Member for Personnel on the Air Council, is particularly revealing. In his memo, which argues against the further recruitment of black or coloured aircrew now that the war had been won, Sir John refers to the 'unsuitability of a gentleman with a name like "U-ba" or "Ah Wong"', or who "looks as though he has just dropped out of a tree", for service in an arm as prestigious as the RAF. While these comments must be read with an eye to the times in which they were written, I suspect that they would have been upsetting to many in Britain, even in 1945.

Only a week after Sir John's missive was sent, on 23 August 1945, an Air Ministry memo (held in PRO AIR 2/13437), no doubt informed by the strongly worded views of Sir John, stated that the Air Ministry would agree to drop the colour bar but that it would now allow a process of 'natural selection' to run its course, whereby, 'on paper, coloured troops (would) be eligible for entry into the service, but the process of selection (would) eliminate them'. This formalized the policy implied by the earlier Air Ministry approach of applying verbal guidelines to exclude black and coloured candidates.

Commenting on the memoranda, Cy Grant wrote that:

> 'These comments … ran counter to the evidence of the general harmony that existed between aircraft crew members, irrespective of their individual race, and to the excellent contribution made by West Indians and West Africans in the RAF.'

Perhaps we should not be surprised that the contribution of the Commonwealth's black and coloured volunteer fliers has been ignored by history, even forgotten. They were, after all, already in the process of being forgotten before their service had come to an end.

Afterword

In 1986, I was a year away from completing a ten year stint as an infantry officer with the Second and Third Battalions, The Jamaica Regiment, part of the Jamaica Defence Force (JDF). Tasked with the interdiction of drug trafficking from and through that island, as well as with confronting armed political gangs in the slums of Kingston, we in the JDF were very conscious of our proud military heritage. Jamaican freedom fighters, known as Maroons and led by the charismatic and fiery 'Nanny', were reputed to have been the first black people to force a peace treaty from the British Army. Samuel Hodge, the second black soldier ever to be awarded the Victoria Cross, Britain's highest award for valour, had served in what was then the West India Regiment, on campaign in West Africa during the colonial period. And, of course, several of us had living relatives who had flown with the RAF during the Second World War. So we knew that, whatever others might like to believe, Jamaicans make excellent soldiers.

In July 1986, I got a very small taste of what the war must have been like for my great-uncle, John Blair. My good friend and colleague, Lieutenant Donald Poulton was the co-pilot aboard a fixed wing JDF aircraft flying a training mission over the island, when his pilot, Captain Harold Wilson, spotted what appeared to be a drug traffickers' aircraft preparing to take off from an airstrip below. Along with another young flier, Lieutenant Dudley Chin, the crew decided that they would land and prevent the drugs plane from departing by blocking the runway. All three men were unarmed, as was their aircraft, and they can only have assumed that their military markings and uniforms would give them sufficient authority to call the trafficker's bluff.

The pilot of the twin engine drugs aircraft, a US citizen and Vietnam War veteran, had other ideas. As soon as he saw that his way was barred, he swung one propeller directly into the JDF aircraft's cockpit. Lieutenant Harold Wilson was later found shredded in two, one half of his body intact and the other half gone forever. Lieutenant Donald Poulton was hanging halfway out of the window on his side of the cockpit, his upper half unblemished, but his body from the waist down burned to a cinder. It was clear that he had suffered terribly.

Lieutenant Dudley Chin survived the incident, but was severely burned about the face, hands and neck. After many months in a burns unit, he returned to flying and I spoke to him briefly a few days after he rejoined his unit and wished him well. Not long after his return to duty a captured drugs aircraft he was piloting back to the JDF airbase crashed and burned. This time Dudley Chin perished in the crash.

Although this represented but a tiny fraction of the cost paid by the airmen of the Royal Air Force, I was hit very hard by these three deaths and they bother me still, almost thirty years later. Great-uncle John and I never discussed these events, but he would certainly have known the full details, for he was at this time the Inspector of Aviation Accidents with the Jamaican Civil Aviation Authority. I believe this knowledge was a key reason for his willingness to share his own experiences with me and, if that is so, then perhaps some small good has come out of things after all.

Appendix 1

List of Coloured Caribbean Volunteer Aircrew
1939–1945

The primary sources for this (still incomplete) list of Second World War Caribbean RAF volunteer aircrew are the records of the Royal Air Force Museum (including, but not limited to, The Nominal Roll of Coloured Candidates, dated October 1944) and two excellent websites; www.caribbeanaircrew-ww2.com and http://www.militarian.com/threads/jamaicans-in-the-raf.2438/.

The Roll of Coloured Candidates is assumed to refer to non-whites only, although this may not be so in every case and it is very possible that there are errors in the tables that follow. Some of the other RAF records examined indicate 'C' (coloured) or 'W' (white) in a number of cases, but many are not so marked. Although men of all races are listed on the websites mentioned, which are regional rather than racial, I have opted to remove those confirmed as white by the RAF from my list for the simple reason that they did not face the colour bar. This by no means detracts from their brave contribution to the Allied victory, but the focus of the book is black and coloured aircrew. I have also left out several men who joined before late 1940, as they are likely to have been Caribbean whites.

The Nominal Roll groups several islands together as the 'Leeward & Windward Islands'. Where I know the particular island of origin, I have indicated that. All the other names are listed under Leeward & Windward.

As the dates of death reveal, at least thirty per cent of these men were killed in action, possibly many more. The research will continue and I hope that one day this list can be completed in full. Anyone interested in obtaining a free electronic copy of my summary list can visit my website at www.markjohnsonbooks.com.

Country	Last name	First name	Born	Killed	Sqn
ANTIGUA					
Antigua	Camacho	Vivian E.	1919		59
Antigua	Henry	John R.			
Antigua	Nanton	Patrick B.		4 Nov 1942	38
Sub-total:			3	Killed:	1
BAHAMAS					
Bahamas	Isaacs	E. A.			
Bahamas	Jordan	Wilbur H.		12 Jun 1943	78
Bahamas	Lightbourn	Warren M.		14 Feb 1945	610
Bahamas	Lothian	Thomas J.		12 Feb 1945	622
Bahamas	Macauley	Frank A. C.		16 Sep 1942	
Bahamas	Maillis	J.C.P.		28 Jun 1943	
Bahamas	Maura	J.			
Bahamas	Moseley	George W.		26 Nov 1944	305
Bahamas	Sawyer	John P. A.		15 Sep 1941	207
Sub-total:			9	Killed:	7
BARBADOS					
Barbados	Aranha	N.F.			
Barbados	Archer	Phillip L. I.		17 Jun 1943	
Barbados	Barrow	Errol W.	1920		
Barbados	Barrow	G. A.		PoW '42	
Barbados	Bauer	F. P.			
Barbados	Carter	Geofrey W.		16 Mar 1944	18
Barbados	Cuke	Mark R.		17 Nov 1941	
Barbados	Cumberbatch	Grey D.	1921	5 Mar 1943	100
Barbados	Cummins	B. A.			
Barbados	Davies	Derek S. B.			224
Barbados	Deane	David S. W.		29 Sep 1943	
Barbados	Dunlop	Andrew P. C.		10 Dec 1942	
Barbados	Edghill	Stanley P.			15
Barbados	Gibson	H. Mc. E.			
Barbados	Gooding	Arthur W.		9 Aug 1943	
Barbados	Hynam	Winston K.			103/100
Barbados	Ince	Clarence D.		22 Jun 1943	7

Country	Last name	First name	Born	Killed	Sqn
Barbados	Inness	Ardel			
Barbados	Inniss	Aubrey	1916		236/248
Barbados	Inniss	George H. F.		4 Jan 1941	106
Barbados	Inniss	Ronald N.			
Barbados	King	Charles P.		26 Jun 1943	9
Barbados	Lynch	Richard C.	1921	17 Sep 1942	501
Barbados	Mahon	Michael S. R.		21 Sep 1944	
Barbados	Manning	Jack H.		5 Jan 1943	117
Barbados	Miller	Bruce F. H.		22 Oct 1943	103
Barbados	Partridge	J. S.			
Barbados	Proverbs	Keith G.		10 Sep 1945	517
Barbados	Skinner	John R.		2 Oct 1945	517
Barbados	Skinner	John W. S.		3 Jun 1944	640
Barbados	Smith	Henry V.		20 Jun 1940	10
Barbados	Walrond	Arthur A.		29 Jun 1943	15
Barbados	Weeks	Arthur O.			132
Barbados	Worme	H. E. S.			
Barbados	Yearwood	Campbell			74
Sub-total:			35	Killed:	19
BELIZE					
Belize	Balderamos	Leo C.			
Belize	Barrow	R. J.			
Belize	Fairweather	Gilbert W.		22 Jun 1944	83
Belize	Grant	C. E. L.		6 Feb 1943	
Belize	Leslie	L. H.			
Belize	Longsworth	L. F.			
Belize	Pinks	C. N. R.			
Belize	Sabido	W. J.			
Belize	Waight	Cassian H.	1912	20 Feb 1944	101
Belize	Wallen	E. E. L.			
Belize	Ybarra	A. T.			
Belize	Zayden	P.			
Sub-total:			12	Killed:	3

Country	Last name	First name	Born	Killed	Sqn
BERMUDA					
Bermuda	Grant Ede	Herman F.		9 Jun 1940	263
Bermuda	Lang	James			105
Bermuda	Richardson	H. C. R.			
Bermuda	Welch	Geoffrey A.		12 Jan 1943	38
Sub-total:			4	Killed:	2
CUBA					
Cuba	Losa	Ricardo		16 Dec 1943	49
Cuba	Taylor	George R. I.			405
Sub-total:			2	Killed:	1
DOMINICA					
Dominica	Alleyne	Osmund		5 Aug 1943	142
Dominica	Bryant	Harold C.		2 May 1944	514
Dominica	Dyrample	Edward S.			
Dominica	McCoy	Lacombe		11 Apr 1943	
Dominica	Plenderlieth	Wallace W.			
Dominica	Severin	Clifford			
Sub-total:			6	Killed:	3
GRENADA					
Grenada	Arthur	Jackson D.		17 Sep 1943	
Grenada	Ferris	John			
Grenada	Greaves	W. G. T.			
Grenada	Marryshow	Julian			602
Grenada	Ross	Colin P.		3 Nov 1943	49
Grenada	Scoon	Jellicoe			41/198
Sub-total:			6	Killed:	2
BRITISH GUYANA					
British Guyana	Alves	E. I.			
British Guyana	Braithwaite	E. R.			
British Guyana	Clavier	A. P.			
British Guyana	Cunningham	Alexander			
British Guyana	De Frietas	J. J.			
British Guyana	De Silva	Desmond M.		24 Aug 1943	218
British Guyana	Fizul-Karim				

Country	Last name	First name	Born	Killed	Sqn
British Guyana	Gonsalves	Frank W.		18 Aug 1945	356
British Guyana	Goveia	A.			
British Guyana	Grant	Cy		PoW '43	103
British Guyana	Grant	M. St. C.			
British Guyana	Griffith	H. J.			
British Guyana	Hall	Ronald			
British Guyana	Haly	Edward F. H.		17 Sep 1944	
British Guyana	Harding	Oscar L. H.		25 Feb 1944	433
British Guyana	Hoban	D. G. H.			
British Guyana	Luck	W. R.			
British Guyana	MacDougal	Ian Neil	1920		
British Guyana	Miller	Cecil H. E.			
British Guyana	McLean	C. A.			
British Guyana	Osborn	F. L.			
British Guyana	Way	Kenneth A.		4 Apr 1943	149
British Guyana	Weston	Frederick T.	1908	31 Aug 1943	
British Guyana	Wood	Thomas R. R.		3 Jun 1942	115
Sub-total:			24	Killed:	7
JAMAICA					
Jamaica	Abbott	Aloysius J.			
Jamaica	Abrahams	T. P.			
Jamaica	Adam	William W.		15 Mar 1940	57
Jamaica	Aiken	Aston K.		8 Aug 1944	107
Jamaica	Aitken	P. T. H.			
Jamaica	Alexander	C. G.			
Jamaica	Almirall	P. D.			
Jamaica	Ashman	Ivan C.		28 May 1945	
Jamaica	Ashman	Roy W.			106
Jamaica	Atherton	C. V.			
Jamaica	Bacquie	P. C.			
Jamaica	Baker	Hugh A. B.		30 Jul 1944	97
Jamaica	Barrett	W. F.			
Jamaica	Barrowes	J. (Jimmy)			
Jamaica	Bartlett	Vivian H.		29 Sep 1943	158

Country	Last name	First name	Born	Killed	Sqn
Jamaica	Barton	S. J.			
Jamaica	Beckford	Victor E.			
Jamaica	Bell	Robert L.			194
Jamaica	Bennett	D. A.			
Jamaica	Bennett	Roy C.			
Jamaica	Bentley	R. C.			
Jamaica	Blair	John J.	1919		102
Jamaica	Bodden	Keith D.			
Jamaica	Bonitto	John			
Jamaica	Bourne	D. A.			
Jamaica	Bourne	Don			
Jamaica	Brandon	D. F. R.			
Jamaica	Bromfield	D. C.			
Jamaica	Brooks	John C.		11 Feb 1944	2
Jamaica	Brown	Peter			
Jamaica	Brown	R. D.			
Jamaica	Bryan	Herman C.			
Jamaica	Bryan	Isaac R.			
Jamaica	Bunting	Vincent	1918		611/132/154/1
Jamaica	Burke	John E.			
Jamaica	Cameron	F. J.			
Jamaica	Capstick	Herbert	1920		236
Jamaica	Carby	Carl C.			50
Jamaica	Cargill	F. D.			
Jamaica	Caryll	Ian B.		29 Jul 1942	156
Jamaica	Causewell	T. C.			
Jamaica	Chance	David E.	1923		603/248
Jamaica	Chevannes	Ralph G.			
Jamaica	Chin	Arthur C.			34
Jamaica	Chin	L. A.			
Jamaica	Chin Hing	C. N.			
Jamaica	Chong	A. C.			
Jamaica	Chong	K. C.			

Country	Last name	First name	Born	Killed	Sqn
Jamaica	Clarke	A. C.			
Jamaica	Cook	Francis S.		26 Feb 1943	103
Jamaica	Cooper	V. H.			
Jamaica	Cousins	A. G. W.			
Jamaica	Crawford	C. E.			
Jamaica	Da Costa	Huntley			
Jamaica	Dawns	Wilfred O.		17 Jan 1945	
Jamaica	De Lisser	Louis S.		20 Feb 1942	
Jamaica	De Souza	Ivor S.	1918		464
Jamaica	Dickson	R. H.			
Jamaica	Dixon	R. G.			
Jamaica	Duncan	Allan U.		2 Dec 1943	9
Jamaica	Dundas	A. T.			
Jamaica	Ebanks	John	1920		571
Jamaica	Eulette	C. A.			
Jamaica	Ferguson	G. W.			
Jamaica	Fielding	C. E.			
Jamaica	Flook	W. A.			
Jamaica	Fonseca	Donald E.		21 Apr 1944	207
Jamaica	Forbes	H. A.			
Jamaica	Forbes	L. G.			
Jamaica	Fox	R. St. J.			
Jamaica	Galbraith	Ivor S. C.		5 Jan 1943	175
Jamaica	Gay	John			
Jamaica	Gordon	Egbert A.	1919	5 Apr 1944	
Jamaica	Gordon	Percival E.		28 Feb 1945	
Jamaica	Grannum	Patrick C.			
Jamaica	Grant	Henry J.		17 Jul 1945	
Jamaica	Guilfoyle	Michael A.	1920		
Jamaica	Hall	J. M.			
Jamaica	Hamilton	John L.		17 May 1943	
Jamaica	Harris	Roy B.		6 Jun 1942	149
Jamaica	Harrison	J. H.			
Jamaica	Harvey	Gilbert W.		19 Mar 1945	

Country	Last name	First name	Born	Killed	Sqn
Jamaica	Hayle	D. E. U.			
Jamaica	Hazell	Vivian B.			576/101
Jamaica	Hearne	J. E. C.			
Jamaica	Henriquez	Alfred G.		17 Aug 1944	630
Jamaica	Hill	G. A.			
Jamaica	Hill	Tony			
Jamaica	Hirst	Harold J.		8 Feb1944	37
Jamaica	Hunter	Robert C.			
Jamaica	Jackson	F. S. I.			
Jamaica	Johnson	A. L.			
Jamaica	Johnson	John R.		31 Oct 1941	76
Jamaica	Jones	K. A. N.			
Jamaica	Ken	K. A.			
Jamaica	Lawrence	Arthur H.		8 Dec 1941	144
Jamaica	Lawrence	J. C.			
Jamaica	Lawrence	R. A. A.			
Jamaica	Leslie	Sefton L.		4 Apr 1945	
Jamaica	Levy	M. H.			
Jamaica	Lightbody	Hugh A.		15 Jul 1944	515
Jamaica	Lindo	C. E.			
Jamaica	Lindo	Harold L.	1917	15 Feb 1944	103
Jamaica	Lindo	Vernon			
Jamaica	Lloyd	Loan A.		24 Sep 1944	247
Jamaica	Lynch	Lincoln O.			102
Jamaica	Manley	Michael	1924		
Jamaica	Marshall	Oliver			
Jamaica	Martin	Ronald B.		11 May 1943	1435
Jamaica	Maxwell	C. A. W.			
Jamaica	McCalla	H. M. F.			
Jamaica	McIntoch	L. M.			
Jamaica	McLaren	H. H.			
Jamaica	Melhado	Leslie S.		6 Jun 1942	44
Jamaica	Mendez	V. A.			
Jamaica	Miller	E. I.			

Country	Last name	First name	Born	Killed	Sqn
Jamaica	Mollison	O. K. A. R.			
Jamaica	Munroe	Stanford A.		5 May 1945	
Jamaica	Murray	R. W.			
Jamaica	Newman	H. O.			
Jamaica	O'Connor	A. D.			
Jamaica	Pearson	Arthur O.		31 May 1945	
Jamaica	Pennicooke	Basil H.			
Jamaica	Philips	C. H.			
Jamaica	Plummer	R. K.			
Jamaica	Pouyat	Taunton O.	1918	7 Dec 1943	
Jamaica	Powell				
Jamaica	Pusey	Lionel L.			
Jamaica	Reid	Arthur G.		21 Nov 1944	10
Jamaica	Reid	Clifford C.			
Jamaica	Richardson	William S.			
Jamaica	Roach	P. A.			
Jamaica	Robertson	James D. A.		1 May 1945	160
Jamaica	Robinson	Phillip		23 Jun 1944	
Jamaica	Robison	Charles			
Jamaica	Robison	Hugh	1920		65
Jamaica	Robison	Jack			
Jamaica	Rodney	A. S.			
Jamaica	Rubie	Robert			
Jamaica	Samms	Clarence			
Jamaica	Samms	L. G.			
Jamaica	Samuda	R. J.			
Jamaica	Saunders	K. D. A.			
Jamaica	Saunders	R. J.			
Jamaica	Scudamore	C. H.			
Jamaica	Shaw	Harry A.			
Jamaica	Smellie	F. H.			
Jamaica	Smith	F. D.			
Jamaica	Smith	M.		PoW 44	
Jamaica	Smythe	Noel B.		26 Jun 1943	196

Country	Last name	First name	Born	Killed	Sqn
Jamaica	Strachan	William A.			99 /156
Jamaica	Sutton Brown	Kenneth E.			
Jamaica	Thomas	Herbert P.		5 Mar 1945	514
Jamaica	Thompson	Dudley L.	1917		
Jamaica	Thorne	Arthur G.		20 Dec 1943	78
Jamaica	Tomlinson	E. R.			
Jamaica	Tucker	Victor E.		4 May 1942	129
Jamaica	Urquhart	T. M.			
Jamaica	Veitch	R.			
Jamaica	Walker	Allan D.		20 Mar 1942	104
Jamaica	Wallace	E. N.			
Jamaica	Wheatley	R. F.		19 Aug 1944	
Jamaica	Wickers	D. S.			
Jamaica	Williams	H. V.			
Jamaica	Williams	Richard U.		26 Sep 1944	183
Jamaica	Wint	Arthur	1920		
Jamaica	Wint	D. H.			
Jamaica	Wint	John Lloyd			
Jamaica	Wong	A. R.			
Jamaica	Wong	Crafton D.		4 Jan 1945	
Jamaica	Wooler	Herbert B.	1920	8 Jan 1942	406
Jamaica	Wynter	Hugh O.			207
Sub-total:			**172**	Killed:	**44**
LEEWARD & WINDWARD					
Leeward & Windward	Bernard	J. C.			
Leeward & Windward	Dalrymple	V. E. G.			
Leeward & Windward	Josephs	J. C.			
Leeward & Windward	Lawrence	E. A. H.		10 July 1944	
Leeward & Windward	Lowhar	G. W.			
Leeward & Windward	Meade	C. N.			
Leeward & Windward	Purnell-Edwards	William P. L.		15 Oct 1944	186
Leeward & Windward	Shillingford	A. J.			
Sub-total:			**8**	Killed:	**2**

Country	Last name	First name	Born	Killed	Sqn
MONTERRAT					
Montserrat	Kelsick	Osmond R.		13 May 1943	175
Sub-total:		1	Killed:		1
NICARAGUA					
Nicaragua	Smith-Vaughan	A. H.			
Sub-total:		1	Killed:		0
PUERTO RICO					
Puerto Rico	Gilormini	Mihiel	1918		346
Puerto Rico	Nido	Alberto A.	1919		
Puerto Rico	Oquendo	William C.	1915	20 Jun 1942	
Sub-total:		3	Killed:		1
ST. KITTS					
St. Kitts	De lisle	Sydney		13 Oct 1944	31
St. Kitts	Vanier	Eugene D.	1916	1 Sep 1942	
St. Kitts	Veira	Basil V. L.	1914	28 Apr 1943	12
Sub-total:		3	Killed:		3
ST. LUCIA					
St. Lucia	Barnard	Donald B.			142
St. Lucia	Du Boulay	Denis C.		24 Aug 1943	426
St. Lucia	Dulieu	Henry E.		22 Nov 1943	83
St. Lucia	Etienne	Hugh T.		5 Mar 1943	214
St. Lucia	Shingleton-Smith	David		1943	
Sub-total:		5	Killed:		4
ST. VINCENT					
St. Vincent	Abbott	Randolph			429
St. Vincent	Osment	David E. T.			150
Sub-total:		2	Killed:		0
TRINIDAD					
Trinidad	Ablack	Lennox			358
Trinidad	Agostini	R. A.		19 Oct 1942	
Trinidad	Alcazar	J. P. C.		14 Apr 1944	851
Trinidad	Alcazar	William E.		30 Jun 1942	405

Country	Last name	First name	Born	Killed	Sqn
Trinidad	Alexander	E.			
Trinidad	Alexander	Kenneth J.		7 Jul 1942	156
Trinidad	Alfred	Joseph M.		26 Feb 1945	75
Trinidad	Alston	James			299
Trinidad	Alston	Michael R.			74
Trinidad	Anderson	Basil C.	1922		218
Trinidad	Anderson	David J.			
Trinidad	Apack	Kenneth			
Trinidad	Archibald	William B.	1915		35
Trinidad	Bahadoor-Singh	A. R. A.			
Trinidad	Bain	Donald A.			
Trinidad	Baker	W. A.			
Trinidad	Belle	J. Fritz			
Trinidad	Bernal	Stanley H.			
Trinidad	Bernard	A. R.			
Trinidad	Bernard	R. A.			
Trinidad	Bowen	Horace G. T.			
Trinidad	Britto	Raymond		2 Jan 1943	
Trinidad	Bruce	A.			
Trinidad	Bryden	Richard A.		4 May 1942	
Trinidad	Bushe	G. W. P.			
Trinidad	Bynoe	E. R.			
Trinidad	Bynoe	Peter C. A.	1918		
Trinidad	Bynoe	Quentin A.			
Trinidad	Carrington	A. John	1919		200/ 223/23
Trinidad	Carrington	Edgill R.		PoW '43	78
Trinidad	Cerny	Karel			
Trinidad	Charles	Hilton D.		27 Apr 1945	228
Trinidad	Chisholm	Rauri			
Trinidad	Cipriani	Mervyn E.		22 Oct 1943	158
Trinidad	Cipriani	Thomas M.		22 Nov 1944	126
Trinidad	Clapperton	C. W.			
Trinidad	Collymore	H. W.			

Country	Last name	First name	Born	Killed	Sqn
Trinidad	Crawford	D. A.			
Trinidad	Critchlow	A. B.			
Trinidad	Cross	Ulric P.	1917		139
Trinidad	Cumming-Bart	Jerome T.		2 Dec 1943	426
Trinidad	De Freitas	Henry A.	1917	6 May 1943	
Trinidad	De Meillac	Guy M.		9 Apr 1943	7
Trinidad	De Meillac	Yves		3 Oct 1943	90
Trinidad	De Verteuil	Desmond			31/ 352/52
Trinidad	De Verteuil	Edmund J.			
Trinidad	De Verteuil	Frank A.			
Trinidad	De Verteuil	Hugh J.			
Trinidad	De Verteuil	Laurant J.			98
Trinidad	De Verteuil	Michael P.			
Trinidad	De Verteuil	Noel			
Trinidad	De Verteuil	P. J.			100
Trinidad	De Verteuil	Peter			
Trinidad	De Verteuil	Roger			
Trinidad	Dempsey	F. J.			
Trinidad	Devaux	Cyril			
Trinidad	Dos Santos	Theophilus		18 Aug 1943	426
Trinidad	Dowdy	Frank			150
Trinidad	Eckel	Cecil			
Trinidad	Elder	Alexander			214
Trinidad	Farfan	Esmond			12
Trinidad	Farfan	Ferdinand			601/145
Trinidad	Fitt	Stanley W.			
Trinidad	Fitzbell				
Trinidad	Ford	G. M.			
Trinidad	Fraser	Alexander		27 May 1944	268
Trinidad	Gaskin	D. S. G.			
Trinidad	Gilchrist	W. J.			
Trinidad	Gilkes	Leslie F.		2 Aug 1943	9
Trinidad	Giuseppi	E. E. L.			

Country	Last name	First name	Born	Killed	Sqn
Trinidad	Gobin	Hugh A. A.			
Trinidad	Gobin	L. A.			
Trinidad	Goddard	C. K.			
Trinidad	Gomez	Vernon P.			95/204
Trinidad	Gordon	John K.			
Trinidad	Gordon	William G.	1914		
Trinidad	Gough	G. B.			
Trinidad	Graham	Ambrose		12 Sep 1944	
Trinidad	Graham	C. W.			
Trinidad	Grant	Kenneth G.		25 Jul 1944	807
Trinidad	Greenidge	John A.		30 Mar 1944	419
Trinidad	Hamel-Smith	Anthony H.	1920		429/608
Trinidad	Harries	Thomas		PoW 44	19
Trinidad	Heath	E. W.			
Trinidad	Hird	John R.			
Trinidad	Horsham	John F.			10
Trinidad	Hosein	Y.			
Trinidad	Howard	G. A. P.			
Trinidad	Hubah	Gilbert C.			168
Trinidad	Hudson	H. N. G.			
Trinidad	Hyde	James J.		25 Sep 1944	132
Trinidad	Ironside	Jim			
Trinidad	Ironside	Willy H.			
Trinidad	Jardine	E. W.			
Trinidad	Johnstone	A.			
Trinidad	Jones	L.			
Trinidad	Joseph	Collins A.		31 May 1944	130
Trinidad	Keating	L. J.			
Trinidad	Kelshall	Arnold S.		PoW '43	254
Trinidad	Kelshall	John B.			
Trinidad	Kelshall	Philip W.			169/29
Trinidad	Kenny	Patrick	1907	2 Nov 1944	195
Trinidad	Kernahan	Kenneth I.		28 May 1944	12
Trinidad	Kerr	C. L.			

Country	Last name	First name	Born	Killed	Sqn
Trinidad	Kerr	Louis N. L.		23 Sep 1943	76
Trinidad	King	Herbert A.		Missing – Apr 44	542
Trinidad	Knox	Harold D.			
Trinidad	Knox	William S.	1924		
Trinidad	Lau	George S.	1921		117/ 353/511
Trinidad	Lennigan	John D.			
Trinidad	Look Yan	Ulric L.		14 Jan 1944	
Trinidad	Lopez	G. P.			
Trinidad	Lucien	G. M.			
Trinidad	Lushington	Claude			
Trinidad	Lyder	Garth			180
Trinidad	Mackay	B. M.			
Trinidad	Maingot	Desmond			
Trinidad	Maingot	Keith			
Trinidad	Marryshow	J. A.			
Trinidad	Marsden	Ken			135
Trinidad	Martinez	Bernard B.			
Trinidad	Martinez	Vincente			
Trinidad	Massiah	C. A.			
Trinidad	Massiah	P. St.C.			
Trinidad	McBride	James M.		17 Dec 1943	161
Trinidad	McDonald	Alexander		12 Feb 1941	
Trinidad	Merry	David		4 May 1944	
Trinidad	Merry	Harry S.			626
Trinidad	Meyer	Thomas H.			155/615/30
Trinidad	Mitchell	M. J.			
Trinidad	Montano	Robert C.	1921		
Trinidad	Murray	Frank			
Trinidad	Murray	Geof			
Trinidad	Murray	Neville			427
Trinidad	Naimool	Elijah			
Trinidad	Noel	Roderick			
Trinidad	Norton	Noel P.	1927		7

Country	Last name	First name	Born	Killed	Sqn
Trinidad	Nunez	George A.		1 May 1943	9
Trinidad	Osborne	Lawrence	1922		
Trinidad	Oxley	Edmund J.			
Trinidad	Pantin	Kenneth J.			
Trinidad	Pemberton	Thomas			
Trinidad	Pereira	Charles V.	1913		139/105
Trinidad	Perera	K. W. M. N.		8 Dec 1942	
Trinidad	Pereira	Roderick N.			83
Trinidad	Peyton	Donald 'Paton'			
Trinidad	Philipps	Robin G.		28 Jan 1944	183
Trinidad	Pitts	Edward R.		7 Nov 1940	70
Trinidad	Pitts	Jack J.			
Trinidad	Pitts	Jim W.			114
Trinidad	Pocock	A. Michael			
Trinidad	Pollard	Ormond E.			12
Trinidad	Pounder	L. A.			
Trinidad	Ramsaran	J. A.			
Trinidad	Rawlins	Kenrick W.		13 Aug 1943	139
Trinidad	Ray	Charles			
Trinidad	Recile	Winston H. E. A.			64/1
Trinidad	Regende	W. M. J.			
Trinidad	Reyes	Claude			
Trinidad	Richards	John L. H.		1 Apr 1945	
Trinidad	Richardson	R.			
Trinidad	Rivero	Vivian A.			47
Trinidad	Rochford	David G.		2 May 1945	618
Trinidad	Rodriguez	Russel			
Trinidad	Rooks	Colin O.		Jun 1944	431
Trinidad	Rostant	Keith J. K.			145
Trinidad	Rother	Louis A.		25 Oct 1943	
Trinidad	Scheult	E.			
Trinidad	Scoon	Jellicoe			41/198
Trinidad	Short	Walter H.		24 Dec 1944	181
Trinidad	Small	Charles W. R.		1 Oct 1944	

Country	Last name	First name	Born	Killed	Sqn
Trinidad	Smith	Alst Claude D.			213
Trinidad	Smith	Louis R. G.			92/80
Trinidad	Sorzano	R. M.			38
Trinidad	Stone	Herbert A.		3 Jun 1943	53
Trinidad	Swan	Christoper			
Trinidad	Swan	G. S. C. G.			
Trinidad	Swan	J. G.			115
Trinidad	Sydney	William			
Trinidad	Sylvester	Oscar O.			15
Trinidad	Tip	Allan P.		5 April 1945	166
Trinidad	Todd	William W.	1913		
Trinidad	Urich	George D.		16 May 1944	18
Trinidad	Venebles	Hugh D.		9 Apr 1943	418
Trinidad	Vilain	F. W.			
Trinidad	Vincent	Claude M.			
Trinidad	Walker	Mark M.			
Trinidad	Wilson	George S.	1922		41
Trinidad	Wilson	John D.		3 Jul 1943	208
Sub-total:			189	Killed:	45
UNKNOWN					
Unknown	Augier	Fitzroy R.			
Unknown	Becherel	R. J.		11 Nov 1944	
Unknown	Corfield	P. B.			
Unknown	Fletcher	Jerry			
Unknown	Grant	Caesar			
Unknown	Huxtable	Robert G.		3 Jun 1944	
Unknown	Johnson	A. S. A		24 Jul 1944	
Unknown	Morrison	R. J.			
Unknown	Ross	J. S.			
Unknown	Ross	D. F. C.			
Sub-total:			10	Killed:	3
GRAND TOTAL			495	Killed:	148

Appendix 2

The Enemy

I originally intended to intersperse the story with notes profiling some of the Luftwaffe pilots who were in the air at the same time as the Caribbean crewmen. I wanted to explain just who the Caribbean men were up against. During my reviews of the text, I realized that this wasn't working as I had hoped. However, I still find the contrast between the experience and proven ability in combat of the German night fighter pilots and the greenness and incongruity of the black volunteers to be breathtaking, so I decided to include my notes as an Appendix for those who might be interested. I also added a paragraph about the Commandant of Stalag Luft III, a very interesting character in the tale.

Oberst Friedrich Wilhelm Gustav von Lindeiner genannt von Wildau
Towards the end of the war, Colonel von Lindeiner, the former Commandant of the Stalag Luft III PoW camp, took the role of second-in-command of a German combat infantry unit. Lindeiner was wounded by Soviet troops on the approaches to Berlin in 1945, but he managed to evade capture by the Russians and later surrendered to the British Army. Imprisoned for two years in the 'London Cage', von Lindeiner testified at the British-led investigation into the unlawful execution of escaped Stalag Luft III prisoners by the Gestapo. It was found that he had followed the Geneva Conventions correctly during his tenure as Commandant of the camp and he was released, based largely on testimony to this effect by former Allied prisoners. Oberst von Lindeiner died in 1963 at the age of eighty-two, his reputation and honour intact.

Günther Bahr

Günther Bahr was born on 18 July 1921, at Neu-Leegden, in the Samland region of Ostpreußen (East Prussia). Bahr joined the rapidly expanding Luftwaffe, the German Air Force, in the late 1930s and by 1941 he had been serving as a flight instructor with a twin engine fighter-bomber school for one year. In December 1941, six months after the German invasion of the Soviet Union, he was transferred to the Eastern front and had his first victory in the air on 4 March 1942, when he shot down a Russian biplane.

At the end of March, Bahr converted to night fighting, meaning that he would now fly specially adapted aircraft to hunt down enemy bombers and intruders in the dark. He was transferred back to Germany where the British night bombing campaign against cities and industry was now gathering pace and becoming increasingly effective.

Bahr claimed his first night victories on the night of 23/24 August 1943, when he first shot down an RAF Stirling and then a Halifax four engine bomber near Berlin. By the end of 1943, Bahr had shot down another seven bombers, taking his tally to ten. These included two USAAF B-17 four-engine bombers, known as Flying Fortresses, which Bahr shot down in daylight over Schweinfurt on 14 October during the second big American raid on the ball bearing plants located in that city. An RAF Lancaster near Hameln on 18 October, a Halifax near Dusseldorf on 3 November, another Lancaster at Hochspeyer on 17 November, and then two more Halifax's and one other unidentified four-engine bomber shot down on the night of 20/21 December completed the total.

By the end of 1944, Feldwebel (Sergeant) Bahr had recorded twenty victories. Then, in the course of only three nights, Bahr claimed a further fifteen kills, including four on each of the nights of 7/8 January 1945 and 28/29 January and seven on the night of 21/22 February. His kills during 1945 comprised four American B 24s and thirteen RAF Lancasters.

Now an Oberfeldwebel (Senior Sergeant), Günther Bahr was awarded the Ritterkreuz (Knight's Cross) on 28 March 1945 for thirty-seven victories. All but one of these had been gained against Allied heavy bombers and he had recorded thirty-four of his kills at night.

Günther Bahr eventually joined the Bundesluftwaffe, part of the post-war German Armed Forces in 1962, retiring in 1975 with the rank of Major. Bahr signed prints for the aviation artist Robert Taylor and many fine examples of Taylor's work can be found on the Internet. These artworks capture the drama and danger of the air war superbly, as well as depicting the special beauty of the natural world fliers inhabit at altitude. Günther Bahr died in April 2009 at the age of eighty-seven.

Georg-Hermann Greiner

Georg-Hermann Greiner was born on 2 January 1920, at Heidenheim in Germany. He joined the German Air Force, the Luftwaffe, in October 1938 and after completing his basic military training Greiner was accepted for flying training. He trained initially with the Luftkriegsschule (Military Flying School) in Berlin, qualifying for his pilot's licence in 30 October 1939. Greiner then attended Flugzeugführerschule (Flight Leaders School) where he was trained to fly multi-engine aircraft. This was followed by Reconnaissance School, Blind Flying School, Dive-Bombing School and finally Fighter Pilots School at Schleissheim. His flying training had lasted more than two years, from March 1939 to September 1941.

In October 1941, Greiner, now a Leutnant, was attached to a squadron based near Hamburg. Along with his unit he took part in Operation Donnerkeil, the aerial protection of the Kreigsmarine battleships *Scharnhorst* and *Gneisenau* during their successful dash through the English Channel from France, to bases in Germany. In April the same year he was promoted to the rank of Oberleutnant. Greiner achieved his first night victory on the night of 25/26 June 1942, when he shot down an RAF Wellington twin-engine bomber over north-west Holland. Many more such victories were to follow.

Georg Greiner recorded his second victory on the night of 6/7 October 1942. He was then transferred to Nachtjadgschule (Night Fighter School) near Stuttgart to undertake night fighter pilot instruction. Following the successful completion of this course, he claimed another victory on the night of 25/26 February 1943, when he shot down an RAF Stirling four-engine bomber near Rastatt. By the end of September, Greiner had thirteen confirmed aircraft kills to his credit.

In the spring of 1944, Greiner flew day missions intercepting US Army Air Force heavy bombers. He claimed victories over four-engine bombers on

30 January and 10 February, and then two more on 6 March. From March 1944, Greiner led 11./NJG 11 and he was awarded the Deutsches Kreuz in Gold on 29 March 1944. Long established as an Ace, Greiner recorded his twentieth victory on the night of 22/23 April and claimed a further two enemy aircraft shot down on the night of 27/28 May. On 27 July 1944, he was awarded the Ritterkreuz, having achieved a total to-date of thirty-six victories.

On the night of 12/13 September 1944, Greiner and his crewman, Oberfeldwebel Kissing, took off from Dortmund to intercept a force of 387 RAF Lancaster bombers, believed to be heading for Frankfurt. RAF losses on many of these night raids were so heavy that German pilots were able to track the path of a raid by the trail of burning wrecks on the ground. However, on this occasion Greiner's own Bf 110 twin-engine night fighter was hit by cannon fire from an intruding RAF Mosquito night fighter moments after take-off. Both sides employed intruder aircraft in an attempt to ambush enemy aircraft as they were taking off from, or landing at, their respective airfields.

Greiner ordered his Oberfeldwebel Kissing to bale out, but Kissing had been severely wounded and could not comply. Greiner then decided to attempt a landing back at his base in Dortmund, despite having one engine on fire. He successfully crash-landed the aircraft, but Kissing had already died from his wounds.

On the night of 7/8 March 1945, Georg Greiner took-off in Bf 110 G-4 (W.Nr. 160 127) to intercept RAF bombers raiding Dessau. Having made no contact with the bombers and beginning to run short of fuel, his aircraft suffered a radio failure. Unable to home in on an airfield he ordered his crewman to bale out. However, Greiner had difficulty exiting the aircraft and hit the rudder badly, injuring his left knee and entangling his parachute in the trailing aerial of the aircraft. He finally managed to free himself and landed near a village in the Eifel region. The injuries he sustained in the incident were sufficient for him to see out the remainder of the war in hospital. He was awarded the Eichenlaub on 17 April 1945, having destroyed fifty-one enemy aircraft.

Following a period of imprisonment by the Allies at a camp in Schleswig-Holstein, Leutnant Greiner was discharged and returned to his mother's home near Stuttgart. Greiner wished to continue in a career involving flying. He and Heinz-Wolfgang Schnaufer decided to try and earn a living flying in South America and on 23 September 1946, set out for Switzerland to contact the relevant consulates to arrange this. However, they crossed the border illegally and were arrested by border guards and interned. Six months later Greiner and Schnaufer were released.

Greiner then moved to Bonn where he studied law. He married in 1949 and became a sales representative for a textile factory. In August 1957 Greiner joined the Bundesluftwaffe with the rank of Hauptmann. He served for another seventeen years, rising to the rank of Oberstleutnant (Lieutenant Colonel), until his retirement in 1972. During the war, Georg-Hermann Greiner flew a total of 204 missions and shot down fifty-one enemy aircraft, of which forty-seven were destroyed at night.

Heinz Rökker

Heinz Rökker was born on 20 October 1920 at Oldenburgh, not far from the Dutch border in northern Germany. He joined the Luftwaffe in October 1939 and began flying training with Flieger-Ausbildungs-Regiment 22 at Güstrow in July 1940. In August 1941, he attended Blindflugschule (Blind Flying School) at Belgrade-Semlin, before completing his training in September 1941 at Nachjagdschule (Night Fighter School) at Neubiberg near München.

Rökker was posted to the Mediterranean theatre on 6 May 1942. On 20 June he shot down an RAF Beaufort twin-engine bomber, by day, over the Mediterranean Sea, while flying from his base at Catania to Kalamaki in Greece. His aircraft was hit twenty-five times by machine-gun fire during this action but he landed safely at the Greek airbase. From bases in Libya he then undertook intruder missions over Egypt, shooting down a total of four RAF Wellington twin-engine bombers during the course of the North African campaign.

On 4 August 1942, Heinz Rökker was transferred to Belgium and he was appointed Staffelkapitän (Squadron Leader) on 15 December 1942. His unit was posted back to the Mediterranean theatre and based in Sicily on 16 February 1943, to face the expected Allied invasion. Rökker undertook night fighter missions over Sicily and Tunisia, recording a RAF Wellington twin-engine bomber shot down near Marsalla on the night of 19/20 April, his sixth victory.

On 2 July 1943, Heinz Rökker led his Staffel back to northern Europe to undertake Reich air defence duties. He enjoyed many successes in the air at this time, claiming three victories on each of the nights of 15/16 March, 22/23 March and 24/25 March 1944, taking his total kills to twenty. He then claimed five British bombers shot down in the area of the Allied landings in Normandy. Now an Oberleutnant (Senior Lieutenant), Rökker was awarded the Ritterkreuz on 27 July 1944. The following night Rökker shot down Lancaster LM206, piloted by Thomas Harvell, who survived, along with one other crew member, near Neufchâteau. The Lancaster crashed into a farm near the River Meuse and one of its engines was displayed in a museum near Neufchâteau. Rökker recorded victory number forty on the night of 7/8 August and on 4/5 November, he shot down four enemy aircraft in the course of the night. Promoted once more – to Hauptmann (Captain) – Rökker shot down two Allied bombers during the RAF raid on Hannover on 5 January (in which John Blair was involved) and then recorded another three victories on the night of 3/4 February, with a further six kills on the night of 21/22 February. He was awarded the Eichenlaub (Oak Leaves) to his Knight's Cross on 12 March for sixty kills. Then, on the night of 15/16 March 1944, Rökker destroyed a final four allied bombers, his last victories of the war, including an RAF Mosquito twin-engine bomber shot down over his own airfield.

Credited with sixty-four victories in 161 missions, Heinz Rökker survived the war and later became a Hauptmann of the reserves in the Bundesluftwaffe. Sixty-three of his kills had taken place at night, including fifty-five four-engine bombers, almost all of these being from the RAF. Rökker and Thomas Harvell, the pilot of Lancaster LM206, shot down by Rökker in 1944, travelled jointly to Neufchâteau after the war to lay a wreath on the graves of the five crew killed during the crash. One other crewman, G. Robinson, survived as a prisoner of war. Rökker and Harvell became close friends and they were both named Honorary Citizens of the city of Neufchâteau in 2006.

Karl-Heinz Scherfling

Karl-Heinz Scherfling was born on 6 September 1918, at Gelsenkirchen in Ruhrgebiet. Scherfling was posted to 7./NJG 1 at the end of 1940. He recorded his first victory on the night of 31 March/1 April 1941, when he shot down a RAF Wellington twin-engine bomber near Groningen. On the night of 9/10 April, he recorded his second, and the Nachtjagd's first victory over a four-engine bomber, when he shot down a RAF Stirling near Lingen. In spring 1942, Scherfling transferred to 5./NJG 2. By the end of 1942, he had increased his victory total to six. On 1 October, 5./NJG 2 was redesignated 10./NJG 1. On the night of 23/24 May 1943, Scherfling claimed two RAF four-engine bombers shot down to record his tenth and eleventh victories. He claimed three RAF Lancaster four-engine bombers shot down on the night of 25/26 June (fifteenth and seventeenth kills). Scherfling claimed his twentieth victory on the night of 13/14 July, when he shot down a RAF Halifax four-engine bomber near Utrecht. By October 1943, Scherfling was serving with 12./NJG 1. He was awarded the Ritterkreuz on 8 April 1944 for twenty-nine victories. On the night of 30/31 March 1944, Scherfling claimed a Lancaster shot down near Venlo to record his thirtieth victory. On the night of 20/21 July 1944, Scherfling recorded his thirty-third, and last, victory. Shortly afterwards, he was shot down and killed by a British night fighter. Scherfling's Bordschütze (gunner) was also killed in the engagement, but his Bordfunker (radio operator) survived, albeit badly wounded.

Karl-Heinz Scherfling was credited with thirty-three victories. All his victories were recorded at night.

Heinz Schnaufer

Heinz Schnaufer was born on 16 February 1922 in Stuttgart. He learned to fly gliders in the late 1930s, these aircraft being the only ones not limited by the treaties signed after Germany's defeat in the First World War. Schnaufer then entered the Luftwaffe as a trainee pilot officer on 15 November 1939, aged just seventeen. Following basic military training and flying training he was promoted to the rank of Leutnant while undergoing multi-engine flying training. After completing his night fighter school, Schnaufer was posted to a squadron based at Stade, near Hamburg. On 15 January 1942, his unit transferred to Saint-Trond in Belgium. Schnaufer's first operational experience came in February that year. His unit was tasked to fly escort for the German navy's capital ships *Scharnhorst*, *Gneisenau* and *Prinz Eugen*, when they successfully broke out from Brest en route for Norway.

On the night of 1/2 June 1942, Schnaufer celebrated his first victory when he shot down an RAF Halifax four-engine bomber near Louvain in Belgium. However, when he attacked a second enemy aircraft, Schnaufer's fighter was hit by return fire and he was wounded in the left leg. After managing to land his damaged plane, he was admitted to hospital for three weeks. By the end of 1942 his victory total stood at seven, including victories over two RAF Wellington bombers and a Whitley V, all recorded on the night of 31 July/1 August.

Heinz Schnaufer had been promoted to the rank of Oberleutnant in July 1943, when his victory total stood at seventeen. He achieved kill number twenty on the night of 8/9 July 1943 and soon afterward he was transferred to a new unit based at Leeuwarden in Holland, where he was appointed Squadron Leader. By 9 October, Schnaufer had recorded his thirtieth victory, and he was awarded the Ritterkreuz on 31 December 1943 for forty-two victories.

Schnaufer's fiftieth victory came on the night of 24/25 February 1944. He was by now an exceptional ace and a deadly menace to any Allied aircrew in his vicinity, and on 1 March 1944, Schnaufer was appointed Gruppenkommandeur of IV./NJG 1, still based at Leeuwarden in Holland. He then shot down five enemy aircraft on the night of 24/25 May to record his seventieth through seventy-fourth victories. Then, on 17 June, he shot down two RAF four-engine bombers, taking his total to eighty.

After destroying a further four RAF heavy bombers on the night of 21/22 June, Hauptmann Schnaufer was awarded the Eichenlaub for eighty-four victories. This award was followed by the Schwertern on 30 July, with his victory total at eighty-nine. In September 1944, his unit retreated into Germany and was temporarily based at Düsseldorf and Dortmund. Schnaufer achieved his 100th victory on 9 October 1944. Still only 22–years-old and one of Germany's leading air combat aces, he was awarded the Brillanten personally by Adolf Hitler on 16 October. Schnaufer was now appointed Kommodore of NJG 4 and at the end of 1944, his victory total already stood at a staggering 106 aircraft kills.

Heinz Schnaufer's greatest success in combat came on 21 February 1945. That day he shot down a total of nine RAF four-engine bombers, two in the early hours of the morning and a further seven, within nineteen minutes of each other that evening. This brought his total kills to 116 aircraft. These planes had contained between 500 and 700 Allied crewmen, representing perhaps one per cent of Bomber Command's total loss of life during the entire war. Twenty-two year old Heinz Schnaufer was now a terrifying killer of men and destroyer of RAF machines, who prowled the night skies over Germany and Holland hungry for more.

Heinz Schnaufer was taken prisoner by the British in May 1945, but was released later that year and returned home to take over the reins of the family wine business. His father had died during the war. After his failed attempt to travel to South America with his close friend Georg Greiner, Schnaufer returned to his wine business, and by 1950 he had built up a very prosperous concern. Then, during a wine-purchasing visit to France, Schnaufer's open top sports car was involved in a collision with a lorry on the main road south of Bordeaux. The lorry had failed to observe the right of way as it entered the main road, some of the heavy gas cylinders it was carrying fell on to Schnaufer's car. Hit in the head, he died in hospital on 15 July 1950, two days after the accident. Schnaufer was twenty-eight.

Heinz-Wolfgang Schnaufer was the top-scoring Nachtjäger of the Second World War. He was credited with 121 kills in 164 combat missions and this total includes 114 four-engine bombers, almost all of them from the RAF.

Bibliography

Interviews

- John Blair; *a recorded interview in Jamaica conducted with Mark Johnson. Also his RAF Logbook, assorted photographs scanned from his personal collection and other miscellaneous notes and remarks between 1996 and 2000.*
- John Ebanks; *a recorded interview in Jamaica, 1997, conducted with Mark Johnson. Also his RAF Logbook, assorted photographs scanned from his personal collection.*
- Donald Jones; *a recorded interview in Jamaica, 1997, conducted with Mark Johnson. Also assorted photographs from his personal collection.*
- Carl Chantrielle; *an interview in Jamaica, 2013, conducted with Mark Johnson. Also, a photograph from his personal collection.*
- Claude Campbell; *interviewed via his nephew on behalf of the author in 2013. Also, a photograph from his personal collection.*

Published sources

- *From Jamaica to Japan*, Thomas S. Forsyth; Yellow Dog ePublishers, 1996
- *A Member of the Royal Air Force of Indeterminate Race*, Cy Grant; Woodfield, 2012
- *The Eighth Passenger* by Miles Tripp; Wordsworth Military Library, 2002
- *Lancaster W4827: failed to return*, Joost Klootwijk; Lilliput Publishers, 2007
- *The RAF Pocklington War Diary*, Mike Usherwood; Compaid Graphics, 1993
- *Lancaster Target*, Jack Currie; Crecy Publishing, 1997
- *The End*, Ian Kershaw; Penguin Books, 2012
- *Men of Air*, Kevin Wilson; Phoenix, 2008
- *Aircrew*, Bruce Lewis; Cassel Military Paperbacks, 2001
- *Bomber Crew*, John Sweetman; Abacus, 2005
- *Tail-end Charlies*, John Nichol and Tony Rennell; Penguin/Viking, 2004
- *Armageddon*, Max Hastings; Macmillan, 2004
- *The Struggle for Europe*, Chester Wilmot; Collins, 1952

- *D-Day*, Antony Beevor; Viking, 2009
- *The Second World War*; Antony Beevor, 2012
- *Our War*, Christopher Somerville; Weidenfeld & Nicolson, 1998
- *For King & Country*, Irving Andre & Gabriel Christian; Pont Casse Press, 2008
- *Hitler's African Victims: The German Army Massacres of Black French Soldiers*, by Raffael Scheck; Cambridge University Press, 2006
- *CHURCHILL'S EMPIRE: The World That Made Him and the World He Made*, Richard Toye; John Macrae Book/Henry Holt & Company, 2010

Online resources
- Aces of the Luftwaffe http://www.luftwaffe.cz/
- 102 (Ceylon) Squadron http://102ceylonsquadron.co.uk/index.html
- Bomber Command http://www.raf.mod.uk/bombercommand/
- RAF Commands http://www.rafcommands.com/
- LuftwaffeClaimshttp://aces.safarikovi.org/luftwaffe.wartime.aerial.victory.credits.html
- Jamaicans in the RAF http://www.militarian.com/threads/jamaicans-in-the-raf.2438/
- Caribbean Studies, Black & Asian History http://www.casbah.ac.uk/index.html
- Caribbean Aircrew in the RAF during WW2 www.caribbeanaircrew-ww2.com/
- www.cieldegloire.com (Broken links at the time of writing)
- uBoat.net http://uboat.net/index.html

Other sources
- 20110330 – MA Essay – Analyse The Contribution of The Commonwealth to Royal Air Force Aircrew in Europe During The Second World War – Wg Cdr Holmes J.
- Archives, The Royal Air Force Museum, Hendon.
- Operational Logs 1939–45, Nos II and IX Sqns, RAF

To see additional images of West Indian aircrew and for links to other online resources, please visit the author's website at www. markjohnsonbooks.com

Index